about WIRE

Shaping wire is a wonderfully versatile medium that you can use to make everything from wire-wrapped bead links to intricate pendants to your own, custom findings.

Shaping wire is available in a range of diameters or "gauges." The lower the gauge, the thicker the wire, so 22-gauge wire is thicker than 24-gauge.

There are different types of shaping wire made from different materials. In this book, we'll use two types of wire:

#1 Artistic Wire is a very malleable, round wire that is available in a multitude of colors and gauges. It is made of copper wire with an enamel color and tarnish resistant coating. The largest diameters are thick enough to use for armature, while the thinnest diameters can be used for crochet.

#2 German-Style Wire is also available in a variety of colors, gauges and shapes. It is made of copper and brass with a tarnish resistant coating and has a temper that's slightly softer than half-hard sterling wire. German-Style Wire can be round, square, half-round or what's called "fancy round"—it looks twisted but the surface is smooth.

How do you choose the right wire for your project? Consider how sturdy the finished design will need to be.

Since German-Style Wire is slightly stiffer than Artistic Wire, you can use it in smaller gauges when you want a delicate effect with added durability. For example, while I would recommend 18 to 20-gauge Artistic Wire for ear wires, it would be safe to use 22-gauge German-Style Wire.

Wire has a natural curve. Regardless of the style of wire you're using, you'll get smoother spirals and loops by working with the curve. You can remove light kinks in the wire by running it through the jaws of flat-nose nylon pliers. Just be aware that straightening the wire is also hardening it slightly, so don't do it too much or the wire will be more likely to break when you bend it.

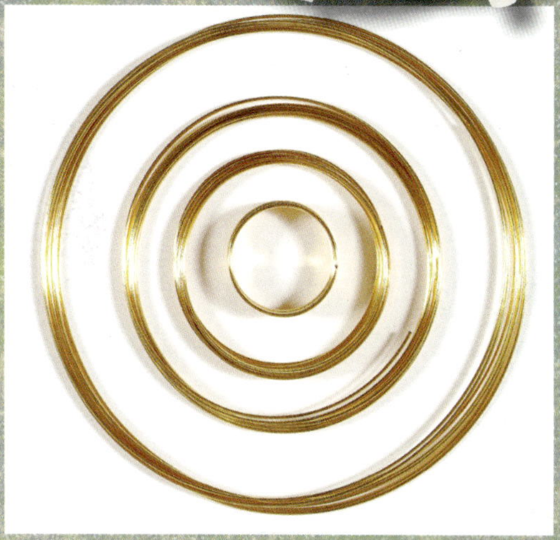

Other STRINGING MATERIALS

ARTISTIC WIRE MESH

With a soft, ribbon-like feel, Artistic Wire Mesh is a gorgeous complement to wire wrapped designs. Its tubular design can be stretched, ruffled, tied, woven and filled to create unusual, eye-catching jewelry.

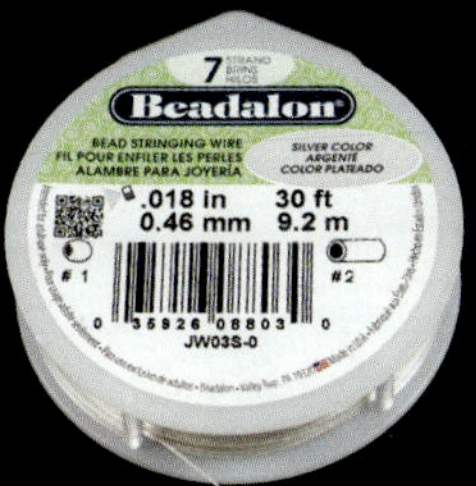

BEADING WIRE

Beading wire combines the strength of stainless steel with flexible, threadlike drape. It is not used for wire wrapping, but it is essential for stringing beaded necklaces and bracelets. Use crimp beads to attach clasp ends and to hold beads in place on the wire.

MEMORY WIRE

Memory wire is tempered stainless steel wire that "remembers" its shape and doesn't require a clasp. Use it for chokers, coiled bracelets, bangle bracelets and rings.

LEATHER CORD

Leather cord is usually round and provides a thick, durable surface for wire wrapping. You can also use it to make simple necklaces for wire-wrapped pendants.

CHAIN

Chain is a popular stringing material that you'll inevitably combine with wirework. Keep different styles in a variety of colors and sizes on-hand for quick and easy necklaces.

Basic TOOLS & more

Many of the projects in this book can be made with a basic set of round-nose pliers, chain-nose pliers and wire cutters. If you want to have a more complete tool kit, though, I recommend adding some of the other tools that will make wirework easier. A crimping tool is essential for stringing necklaces and bracelets.

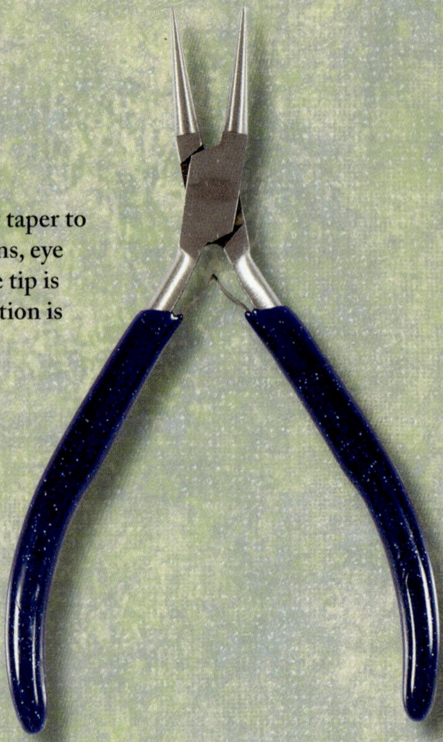

ROUND NOSE

Round-nose pliers have conical tips that taper to points. They're used for looping head pins, eye pins and wire. The narrowest area on the tip is used for small loops while the widest section is used for large loops.

CHAIN NOSE

Think of chain-nose pliers as an extension of your hand! Use them for gripping, making right angles and to open and close loops and rings. The jaws are smooth on the inside and the domed tips taper to a point.

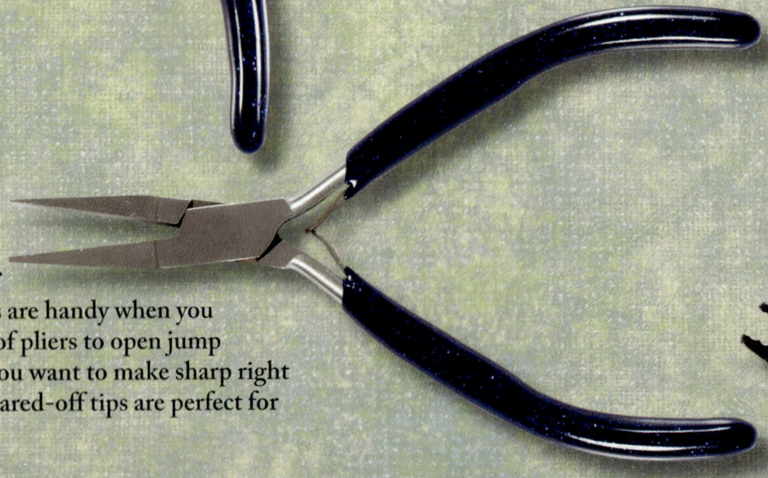

FLAT NOSE

Flat-nose pliers are handy when you need two pairs of pliers to open jump rings or when you want to make sharp right angles. The squared-off tips are perfect for gripping wire.

WIRE CUTTERS

Wire cutters are necessary for cutting shaping wire, head pins, eye pins and beading wire. Sharp, pointy tips allow you to get into tight spaces. For close cuts, hold the flat side of the blades against the work.

CRIMPING TOOL

The crimping tool is designed especially for securing crimp beads to beading wire. Although it isn't used with shaping wire, you'll need it when mixing bead stringing with wirework.

Technique: USING A CRIMPING TOOL

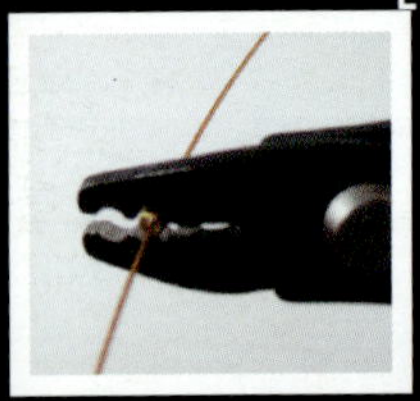

1 Place the crimp bead in the inner jaws on the crimping tool. Squeeze hard to make a crease.

2 Turn the crimp bead 90° and place it in the outer jaws on the crimping tool. Squeeze gently to fold the crimp in half.

3 After adding a bead and a second crimp bead on the wire, use the outer jaws of the tool to add a crimp cover over each crimp bead, if desired.

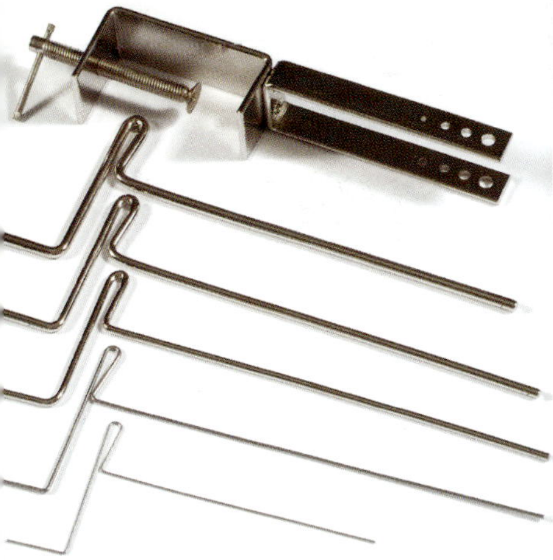

WIRE COILING GIZMO

The Wire Coiling Gizmo has a bracket that attaches to your worktable and a collection of rods, or mandrels, in different sizes that you use to coil wire quickly and easily. See page 25 for instructions.

WIRE ROUNDER

Also called a cup burr, a wire rounder is handy for smoothing wire ends to prevent snags. You could also use a file or emery board for the same purpose.

MEMORY WIRE SHEARS

Some of the projects in this book are strung on memory wire, which requires special shears. Don't attempt to use regular wire cutters with memory wire because it will leave notches in the blades.

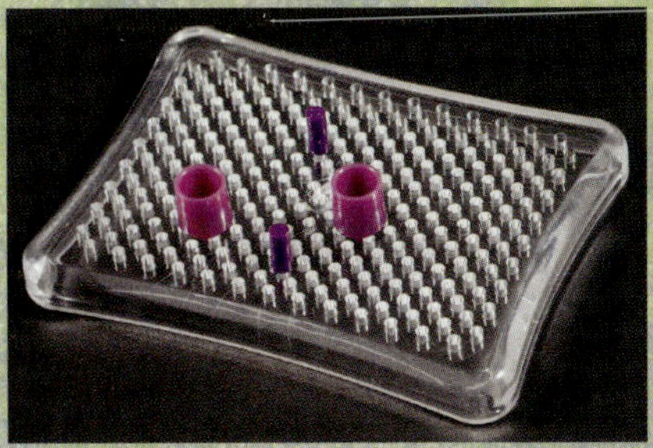

WIRE JIG

There are many different styles of wire jigs. Most have removable pegs that you can position in different places on the grid. Use a jig with 18-gauge to 22-gauge wire to make your own wire motifs.

NYLON JAW PLIERS

Available in a variety of styles, nylon-jaw pliers have protective coverings over the tips that prevent them from making marks on the wire. When the tips get worn out, you can replace them with new ones.

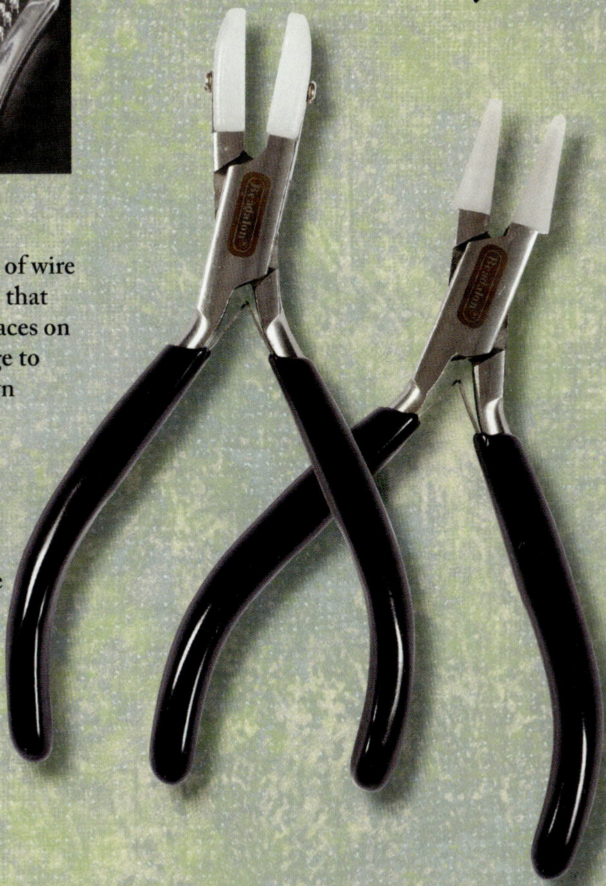

BENT CHAIN-NOSE PLIERS

Like chain-nose pliers, except the tips bend in a curve at the end to get into extra tight spaces. Some people like to use these as their second pliers when opening jump rings and loops.

HAMMER & BENCH BLOCK

Use a hammer and bench block (or anvil) to work-harden wire so it will hold its shape when making spirals, ear wires and other wire motifs. The broad, flat surface flattens wire, while the rounded surface creates texture. Some hammers have nylon heads that protect the plating on the surface of the wire.

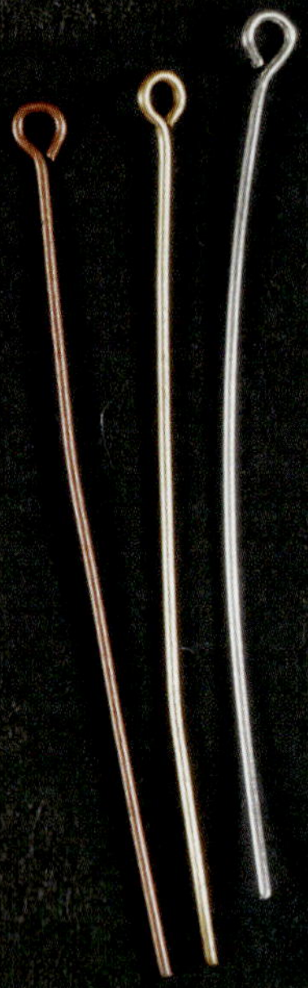

EYE PINS

An eye pin has a loop on the end that can be connected to other components. It's easy to make your own eye pins from 18 or 20-gauge wire (see pages 8-9) but pre-made eye pins are tempered to hold their shape at smaller gauges.

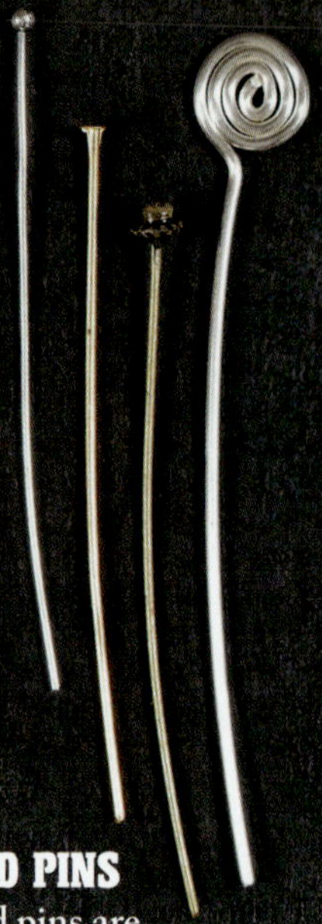

HEAD PINS

Head pins are thin pieces of wire that have a stopper on one end. The stopper can be a basic nail head, a ball or other decorative element. They are available commercially in a wide range of styles. See page 14 to make spiral head pins.

EYE CRIMPS

Eye crimps have a hanging loop and two metal flaps that fold-over to hold cord or wire mesh in place. They're also called fold-over cord ends.

SOLID RINGS

Don't confuse solid rings with jump rings! Solid rings don't have seams and cannot be opened to connect components together. But, they make attractive links and can double as spacer beads.

Basic FINDINGS

"Findings" is a general term that refers to the basic items jewelry makers use to connect things together, make dangles, add length, and more. Each of these components is available in a variety of sizes, styles and colors. In general, choose a finding that is proportionate to your overall design.

JUMP RINGS

Jump ring are single wire circles that connect jewelry components together. They are available in many different sizes and metallic finishes. Or, you can make your own by coiling a length of wire and cutting the rings apart.

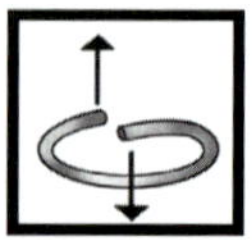

Always open jump rings as shown instead of pulling the ends directly apart like a book. Use pliers to pull one end toward you while pushing the other end away from you. To close the ends securely, brush them past each other and listen for a little "click," then bring the ends back together.

CLASPS

Clasps come in a range of sizes and styles, from lobster claw to toggle. In general, choose a clasp that suits your jewelry. For toggles, make sure the beads near the toggle bar are small enough to allow the bar to pass through the ring. Lobster claw and spring ring clasps are unobtrusive and can be fastened anywhere along a chain. You can make a wire hook clasp to match the wire in your design.

Technique: MAKING YOUR OWN HOOK CLASP

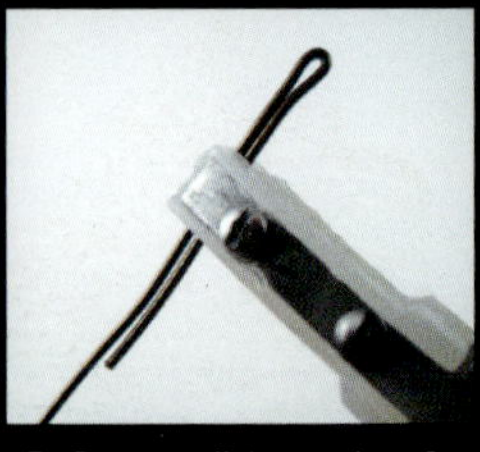

1 Cut a 3" length of wire and fold it back by 2".

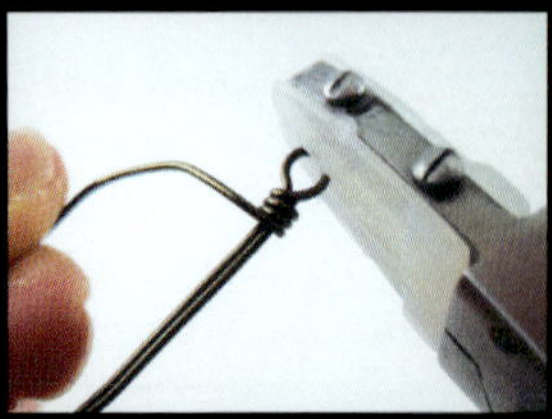

2 At the other end of the wires, use the single wire to make a wrapped loop (see page 10) around the folded wires.

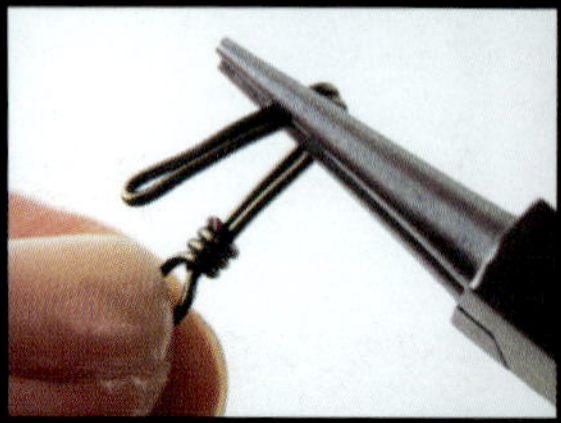

3 Fold the doubled wires in half to form a hook.

4 Use round-nose pliers to bend the end of the hook upward.

CRIMP BEADS

Crimp beads are tiny metal beads that flatten when squeezed with pliers or a crimping tool. Use them to connect beading wire ends or to hold beads in place on beading wire. Refer to the product packaging to see which size crimps go with the beading wire you're using for any given design. Special findings called EZ-Crimps™ are similar but crimp directly to the wire and have a built-in loop (not pictured).

EARRING FINDINGS

There are many different styles of pre-made earrings, or you can make your own. Some things to think about are: How much length you want to add (or not add) with the ear wire, if you want the ear wire to be decorative or plain, which direction the attachment loop needs to face, how secure the ear wire needs to be. Keep any metal allergies in mind when choosing or making earring findings.

MAKING YOUR OWN EAR WIRE

Many people make their own ear wires because they want to completely customize their earrings or because they want sterling silver or gold-filled ear wires. It's quick and easy to make your own—you could substitute them for any of the earrings in this book.

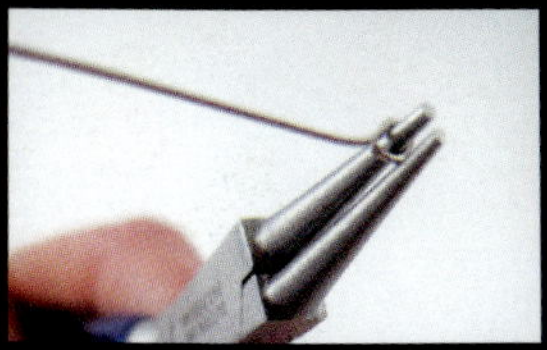

1 Cut a 3"-4" length of 20-gauge wire and make a basic loop (see pages 8-9) on one end.

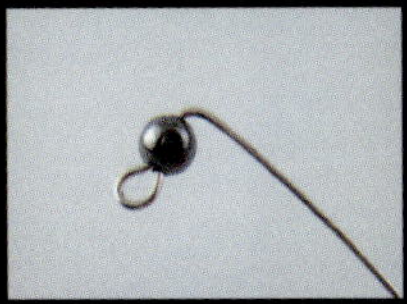

2 Pass the wire through a 4mm round bead or other embellishment and make a right angle.

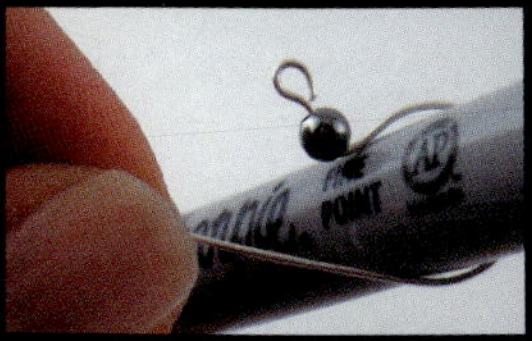

3 Wrap the wire in a large loop around a mandrel (I used a permanent marker) to form the hook.

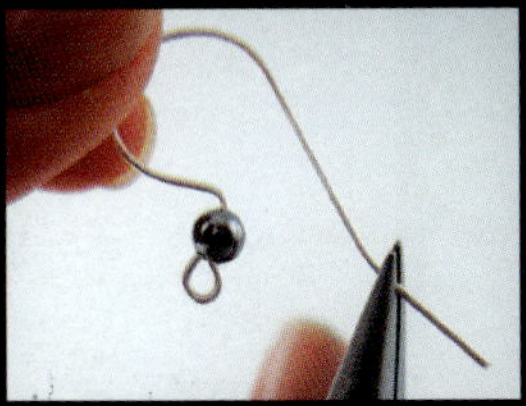

4 Use chain-nose pliers to make a slight angle in the wire.

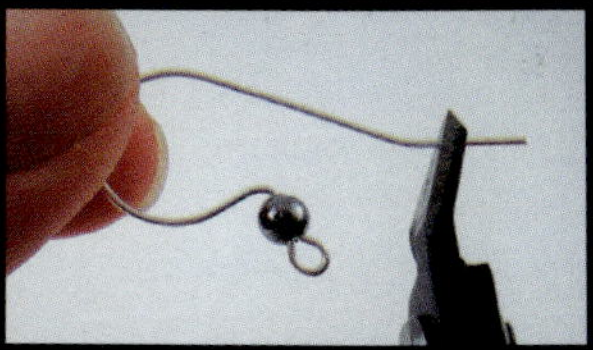

5 Cut off any extra wire. If this wire end is sharp, you can file it with a metal file or emery board.

Specialty FINDINGS

Here are some special findings that you can use to connect things together, add decorative touches or highlight special beads. They add a designer touch to wire-wrapped jewelry designs. Each of these findings comes in different styles and finishes.

BEAD CAPS

Bead caps fit onto beads like little hats. You can use a single bead cap on top of a bead or you can sandwich a bead between caps for a more decorative effect.

BEAD CONES

Typically used to cover the ends of multiple-strand necklaces, bead cones can also be used as tassel toppers and other earring components. Fit them over the pointed ends of teardrop beads for simple, elegant dangles.

KATIEDIDS™ CHANNEL FINDINGS

I developed Katiedids™ channel findings to give beaders the power to customize their designs, right down to the findings. These components act as channel settings for 4mm round beads.

BEAD FRAMES

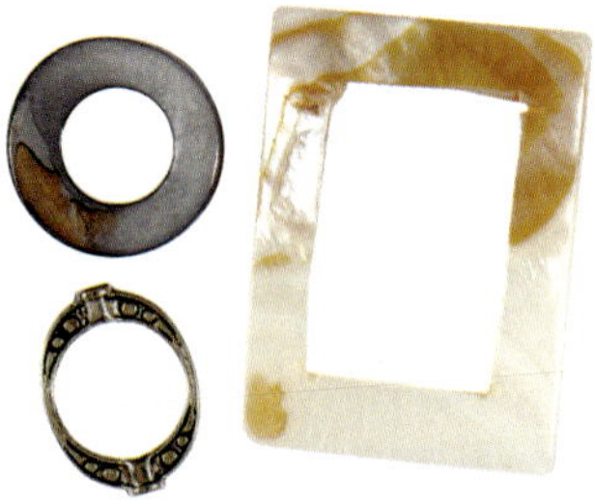

Bead frames are made from a variety of materials and essentially frame beads inside the negative space. Use them to turn plain beads into decorative elements.

SLIDERS

Made from metal or stone, sliders have two sets of holes and are typically used to create double-strand designs. With a little bit of wirework, you can also use them as pendants and earrings.

FILIGREE

Stamped metal filigree can be used as is, but I like layering several pieces together to create unusual pendants and earrings (see pages 20-21).

Types BEADS

Although you can create beautiful jewelry that's completely made from wire, I like to add beads to wire designs for color, depth and style. You'll find a wide variety of beads in this book, from crystal to wood, stone to metal and more. Here's an overview of the types and shapes of beads I used. When substituting beads, keep in mind the overall dimensions of the suggested beads so you can create a similar look.

STONE

From natural stones like jasper and garnet to dyed stones like howlite and magnesite, stone beads are probably the most traditional counterpart to wire-wrapped designs. They give wire designs a natural, organic look.

METAL

Metal beads make great accent or focal beads. However you use them, they add a designer touch and really highlight the other elements in the jewelry. It's trendy to mix hues of gold, copper, silver and hematite.

WOOD

Wooden beads add a warm feeling to wire jewelry. They're available in many different shapes and shades. Like ceramic beads, they often have larger holes that work particularly well with larger diameters of wire.

PEARL & SHELL

Freshwater pearls are easy to identify, but many other types of beads are made from mother-of-pearl and other shells. Pearls and shell beads have a luminous quality that looks beautiful with shiny, metallic wire.

CERAMIC

Earthy and colorful, ceramic beads are a natural fit for wire designs. Many ceramic beads have slightly larger holes that work well with larger diameters of wire.

CRYSTAL

Crystal is highly faceted, leaded glass with lots of sparkle and shine. Swarovski Elements come in a variety of shapes from bicone (like the blue and green beads) to briolette (like the pink bead above).

GLASS

Smooth or faceted, shiny or matte, glass beads are available in a huge variety of colors, shapes and sizes. Aurora Borealis (AB) finish is the rainbow hue that you sometimes see on the surface of glass beads.

Shapes

ROUND
The most basic bead shape, round beads often form the base of an earring design. Mix rounds with other shapes for more texture.

BICONE
A bicone looks like two cones that are connected at their wide ends with the points extending outward. The pointed shape of a bicone adds texture and interest to simple earring designs.

RONDELLE
A rondelle looks like a round bead that has been squashed from end to end. It's wider than it is tall and can be smooth or faceted.

SPACER
This is a general term which refers to flat metal beads that add texture and interest to jewelry designs.

SEED
Seed beads are available in different sizes. The most common are 10/0 and 6/0, with size 6 being larger than 10.

TEARDROP
Narrow at the top and wide at the bottom, these can be drilled across the top of the point or from end-to-end. Faceted teardrops are commonly called "briolettes." They can be flat or three-dimensional.

NUGGET & CHIP
Nuggets have a natural-looking shape and can be flat or three-dimensional. Chips are similar but smaller. When choosing nuggets for earrings, be sure to pick beads with the same length.

RECTANGLE
Flat, rectangular beads are easy to find in a variety of sizes and colors. Use them to add visual interest to simple earrings by mixing them with rounds, bicones or rondelles.

OVALS
Most ovals are flat, but some are more three-dimensional. Flat ovals are perfect for making beaded flower petals.

FACETED
Facets are small cuts on the surface of a bead that reflect light and cause beads to sparkle more than their smooth counterparts. Faceted beads come in many shapes but the most common shape is round.

COIN & LENTIL
Coins and lentils are disk-shaped beads with holes that extend from one end to the other. Coins have thicker edges, while lentils have edges that taper.

Basic WIRE LINKS

Basic loops are quick, convenient ways to connect things together. Be sure to use eye pins or wire in a heavy-enough gauge that the loop won't accidentally pull open.

(1) For the fuchsia earrings: Use 18-gauge wire to make a basic loop and attach it to a 20mm solid ring. Pass the wire through a 5mm spacer, 10mm fuchsia round, 5mm spacer and make another basic loop. Connect the upper loop to an ear wire. Repeat for a matching earring.

(2) The purple necklace uses similar loops and links. Use 18-gauge wire to make eight spacer/10mm light purple/spacer links. For three links, cover the ends of a dark purple bead with bead caps. Connect the bead links together as shown. Attach a length of chain to each end of the necklace to achieve the desired total length. Attach a clasp to one end. For instructions to make a clasp, see page 4.

(3) For the gray earrings: Pass a head pin through a 6mm faceted bead, make a basic link and attach it to an ear wire. Pass an eye pin through the lower holes on a bead frame, a 8mm faceted bead, the upper holes on the bead frame and make a basic loop to attach it below the first bead link. Pass an eye pin through a silver spacer, 8mm glass nugget, silver spacer and make a basic loop to attach it below the previous link. For the lower dangle, pass a head pin through a 10mm faceted round and make a wrapped loop (see pages 10-11) to connect it to the bottom of the earring. Repeat for a matching earring.

MAKING A BASIC LOOP & LINKING TOGETHER

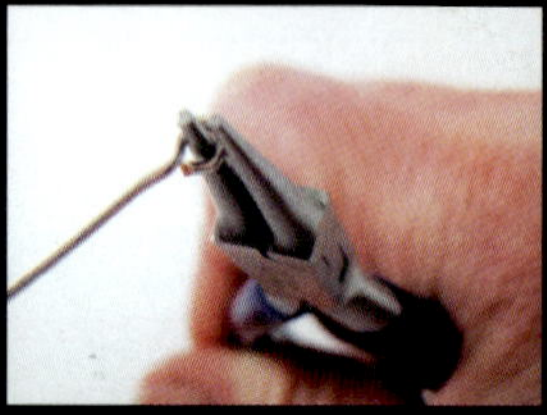

1 Use round-nose pliers to make a loop at the end of a piece of wire.

2 Pass the wire through a spacer, a bead, another spacer then bend it against

3 Trim the wire to a finger's width.

(4) For the heart necklace, combine ceramic, metal and stone beads with leather cord for an easy, casual look: Pass an eye pin through a 10mm rondelle, spacer, 10mm coin, spacer and 10mm rondelle then make a basic loop to attach it to the center of a length of dark brown suede cord. Pass an eye pin through a bead cap, 12mm brown round and a bead cap. Make a basic loop and attach it to the previous link. For the heart, pass a head pin through a rondelle, the 30mm stone bead and make a wrapped loop to attach it to the bottom of the pendant. Knot the cord ends.

(5) Bead caps make the red bracelet stand out. Use 18-gauge wire to make 10 red bead links with bead caps covering the ends of 10mm glass beads. Make a single bead link with 6mm spacers sandwiching a red 18mm floral bead. Connect half of the bead cap links to each side of the large red floral bead, then connect a clasp to one end.

(6) The amber glass necklace uses color to create a cohesive look for beads of different shapes and sizes. For the pendant: pass a head pin through a 15mm bead and the upper hole on a large shell bead frame. Make a large wrapped loop. Use eye pins to make bead links from an assortment of 24 white shell beads and amber glass 8mm-15mm beads. Connect half of the beads to each side of the pendant, then attach a clasp to one end.

Tip

Because basic loops are easy to open, you can make a lot of them, then plan your pattern and connect them together afterward.

4 Use round-nose pliers to roll the wire back toward the stem and to

5 For the next bead link, make a basic loop and open it to attach to the

6 Pass the new wire through a spacer, a bead, a spacer and make a basic loop to

Technique:

MAKING A BASIC LOOP & LINKING TOGETHER

Wrapped LOOPS & LINKS

(1)

(2)

(3)

Wrapped loops and links make decorative, durable connections. They're impossible to open.

(1) Wrapped loops are essential for thin head pins like the ball head pins on the blue earrings. Pass a head pin through a 6mm blue round, spacer, the upper hole on a bead frame, spacer and 4mm blue round. Make a wrapped loop to attach it to the end of a 1" length of chain. Connect the upper link on the chain to an ear wire. Repeat for a matching earring.

(2) The green bracelet features wrapped loop dangles and links. Cut a 3" length of 20-gauge wire and make a wrapped loop on one end to attach it to the circular toggle ring. Pass the wire through a green rondelle, then make another wrapped loop. Make nine more green bead links connected in a chain, then use a small gold bead to make the last link and attach it to the toggle bar. (The small bead allows the bar to pass through the ring and to fasten the clasp.) Make an additional green link and attach it to the toggle ring using two jump rings. Make three antique gold head pin dangles and connect them below the green bead link.

(3) For the mixed metallic earrings: Cut two ¾" lengths of small cable chain. Cut 6" of 22-gauge wire and make a wrapped loop on one end to attach it to one piece of chain. Pass the wire through the hole on one end of the curved channel component, then pass through eight 4mm rounds. Pass the wire out the other end of the channel, make a wrapped loop to connect it to another piece of chain. Pass a head pin through a round bead, spacer, diamond-shaped bead, spacer, round bead and make a wrapped loop. Thread the free end of a chain, the head pin loop and the other chain onto a jump ring. Connect the jump ring to an ear wire (see page 4). Repeat for a matching earring.

MAKING A WRAPPED LOOP & LINKING TOGETHER

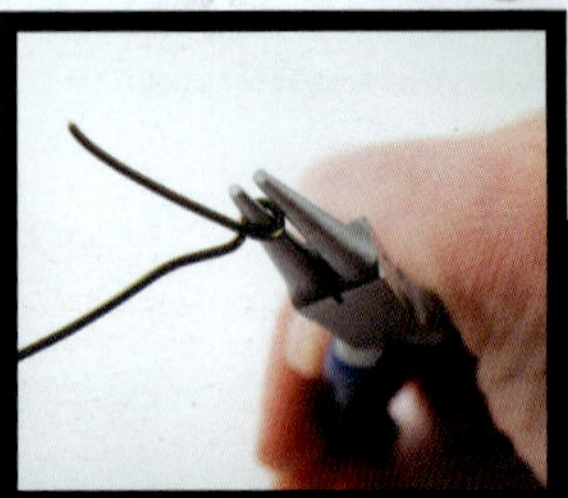

1 Use round-nose pliers to make a loop about 1" from the end of a piece of wire.

2 Coil the short wire around the base of the loop and cut away any excess.

3 String a bead onto the wire, then make another wrapped loop.

(4) The red earrings show how you can make small bead caps by coiling extra wire around the base of the loops. Cut a 6" length of gold 20-gauge wire and make a wrapped loop to connect it to an ear wire. String a large floral bead onto the wire, then make another wrapped loop. Once the bead is securely held in place by the loops, coil the extra wire on both ends around the base of the loop. Connect a ½" length of chain to the lower loop. Pass a head pin through a teardrop bead and make a wrapped loop to connect it to the end of the chain. Repeat for a matching earring.

(5) For the purple earrings: Cut three 1" lengths of small cable chain. Cut a 4" length of hematite wire and make a wrapped loop on one end to connect it to an ear wire. Pass the wire through one end of a bead frame, a 10mm purple bead, the other end of the bead frame. Make a wrapped loop to attach the lengths of chain. Repeat for a matching earring.

(6) Wrapped links make it easy to connect odd-shaped beads like the white stone nuggets. Make five linked nuggets, then make three spacer/10mm red/spacer links alternating with white nuggets. Five nugget links complete the other end of the necklace. Attach a clasp to one end. For the petite red dangles: Pass a head pin through a 4mm faceted red stone bead and make a wrapped loop; repeat 18 times. Connect three dangles to a jump ring and connect to the loops between the red and white beads. Repeat for each set of three dangles.

Tip

Since you won't be able to open the links once they're connected to each other, be sure to plan your design before you begin making links.

4 When connecting two bead links together, slip the new loop onto the previous link before wrapping it shut.

5 Pass the new wire through a bead, make a wrapped loop and trim off any extra wire.

Technique:

MAKING A WRAPPED LOOP & LINKING TOGETHER

Decorative WRAPS

> **Tip**
>
> Everyone forgets to connect wrapped links from time to time. If you have enough beads to complete the design without it, then set the extra link aside and use it for an earring or a link in another project.

Decorative wraps are an extension of the wrapped loop technique on the previous page. Use decorative wraps to connect and embellish bead links or pendants and to add an artistic, handmade touch to wire wrapped designs.

(1) The purple earrings are an easy place to start. Cut a 5" length of 22-gauge fancy round silver wire and make a wrapped loop (see pages 10-11) to attach it to an ear wire. Follow the instructions in the steps below to make a decorative wrapped link. Pass a head pin through an 18mm heart bead and a purple seed bead, then make a basic loop to connect it to the wrapped bead link. Coil any leftover wire around the ear wire to embellish it. Repeat for a matching earring.

(2) Wrapped links are one of my favorite ways to show off multi-color beads. If you look closely at this bracelet, you'll see that it doesn't have accent or spacer beads. The highlighting is all done with the decorative wraps. To figure out how many beads you'll need, wrap the strand around your wrist and add three inches to account for the wire wrapping. Follow the steps below to link the beads together with 22-gauge wire, attaching the clasp to the last link.

(3) Bead caps are another way to highlight multi-color beads. Make the wrapped loop links from 20-gauge wire, then create an eye-catching wrapped pendant. Instead of wrapping wire all the way around the bead, I just crossed it diagonally on the front and back. If you use unsoldered chain, you can open the links and attach them below the pendant and to the ends of the necklace after the loops are wrapped. Otherwise, remember to add them before wrapping the loops shut.

1 Make a wrapped loop on one end of the wire, pass it through a bead and make another wrapped loop but don't cut off any extra wire.

(4) The nugget necklace shows another way to use decorative wraps to highlight special beads. Use 8" lengths of 20-gauge gunmetal wire to make decorative wraps on three 20mm quartz nuggets. Use 3" lengths with antique gold spacers sandwiching 15mm agate coins and wrapped loops to connect the nuggets together. On each end of the necklace, attach three cube/agate/cube links and five 8mm round clear links. Attach a clasp to one end.

(5) For the channel-set earrings: Cut one 8" length of 22-gauge fancy round silver wire. Make a wrapped loop to attach it to an ear wire. Pass inward through a hole on the rectangle, string eight 4mm agate rounds inside the channel, then outward through the opposite end and make a wrapped loop. Wrap the extra wire around the rectangle three or four times to reach the other end. Coil the end around the base of the original loop to secure it. Attach a bead cap/8mm bead/head pin dangle below the channel. Repeat for a matching earring.

(6) Decorative wire wraps add artistic flair to simple drop pendants like the red necklace, which is built from the bottom to the top. String three 8mm red carved stone beads onto individual head pins. Add a 3mm antique gold round to each and make a basic loop (see pages 8-9). Cut a 6" length of fancy round antique brass wire and make a wrapped loop to connect it to the three head pin dangles. Pass the wire through a large-hole antique brass bead that partially covers the loop. Pass through a 20mm red lentil bead and make a wrapped loop to attach it to a necklace chain. Wrap the extra wire downward around the lentil and coil it around the base of the bead, tucking the end inside the antique gold bead.

Splendid SPIRALS

Spirals are ancient symbols and also happen to be one of the first design motifs that most beginning wire workers learn to make. Some scholars think early stone carvings of spirals may represent the sun. Use them to add a style that's both ancient and modern to dangles, wire wraps, the ends of head pins and more.

(1) Spiral head pins make for quick and easy earrings. Cut a 6" length of 20-gauge wire and see the steps below to shape it into a spiral. Make a right angle, then pass through a clear seed bead. Cut a 1" length of wire and coil it (see pages 10-11) three times above the bead (cut off any excess from the coil). Pass the spiral head pin wire through an 8mm light gray bead and make a basic loop (see pages 8-9) to attach it to an ear wire. Repeat for a matching earring.

(2) For freeform spirals: Cut a 5" length of 20-gauge wire and use chain-nose pliers to fold the end back 1/16". Pass through a 6mm round bead, then hold the bead between your thumb and forefinger to form the wire in a three-turn spiral. Bend the wire in a right angle and pass through a 6mm faceted bead and make a basic loop to attach it to an ear wire. Hammer the outer edges of the spiral lightly to keep its shape.

(3) You can use spirals to make quick and easy pendants. For the black necklace: Cut a 12" length of 18-gauge wire and use it to form a 5-turn spiral. Make a right angle, pass through a 22mm onyx diamond-shaped bead, then make a wrapped loop. Coil the extra wire downward over the top of the bead and form the wire end into a spiral. Use a 20mm flat teardrop to make a decorative bead link (see pages 12-13) and top it with a capped bead link. Attach the pendant to the center of a necklace chain.

(4) Spiral links are an interesting way to link beads and provide another way to incorporate this popular motif into your jewelry. For the bracelet, use 22-gauge gunmetal wire to make five spiral links. String six multi-color fresh-water pearls onto individual eye pins and make a basic loop on each. Use the beaded eye pins to connect the spiral links in a chain. Attach a clasp to the last eye pin link.

Technique: MAKING A FLAT SPIRAL

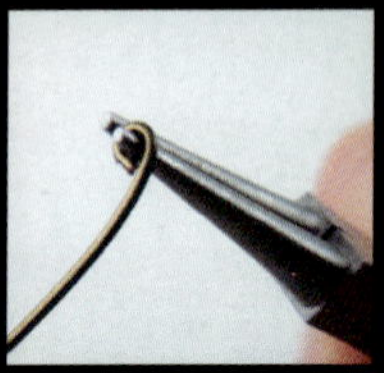

1 Use round nose or chain nose pliers to make a small loop or fold at the end of a piece of wire.

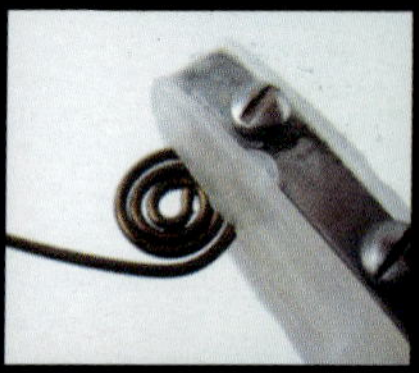

2 Grasp the loop or fold inside the flat plane of chain-nose pliers and turn your wrist to form a spiral. Continue turning until the spiral reaches the desired size.

3 Bend the end in a right angle to create a head pin or dangle, then tap the spiral lightly with a hammer so the spiral will keep its shape.

(5) Use spirals to dress up any bead with a flat surface, like I did with the gray necklace. Cut a 6" length of 20-gauge wire and make a basic loop on one end. Pass it through a silver spacer bead and a 25mm light gray oval. Make a wrapped loop (see pages 10-11) to attach it to the center of a necklace chain in the desired length, then bring the extra wire to the front of the bead and coil it into a spiral. Use a nylon hammer to lightly tap the spiral and work-harden it slightly against the bead. Pass a head pin through a 10mm dark gray bead and make a wrapped loop to attach it below the oval bead. Make two more of these spiral bead dangles and attach each one about 2" away from the center pendant on the necklace. Attach an 8mm light gray beaded head pin to the end of a 1" length of chain; repeat for four dangles total. Attach them as shown on each side of the spiral bead dangles.

(6) The pink necklace combines spiral head pins with a variety of beads for a clustered, cascading effect. First, connect a 3" length of chain to the center of a black leather cord necklace. Pass a head pin through a 40mm magenta stone teardrop and 8mm black rondelle, then make a basic loop to attach it to the chain. Make two more teardrop dangles and attach them evenly spaced on the chain. Pass a head pin through each 12mm faceted round and 7mm spacer bead, make a wrapped loop to attach the dangles evenly spaced on the chain. For the three black bead/spiral dangles, use 5" lengths of 20-gauge wire with 12mm teardrop beads and 3mm silver rounds. Make basic loops to attach them evenly spaced on the chain. For the three silver spiral dangles, use 5" lengths of 20-gauge wire with spacer beads and make basic loops to attach them to the chain.

Tip

You can make decorative spirals from any gauge wire, but spirals made from larger gauges have more structural integrity and can stand on their own.

Technique: FOR A SPIRAL LINK

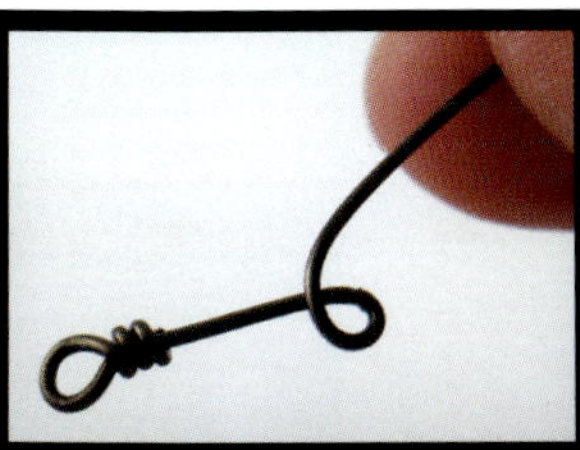

1 Start out with a wrapped loop on one end, then leave a space the size of the desired spiral and fold the wire to make a loop.

2 Form the wire into a spiral around the loop.

3 Open the last loop and attach it to a copper ring.

Beaded PENDANT BAILS

Teardrops, briolettes and other pendants often have holes that go from side-to-side instead of end-to-end. This type of hole requires a special connection to allow the pendant to hang straight instead of at an angle as it would if you simply attached it using a head pin.

(1) For the black necklace, use 22-gauge wire with 20mm black pointed pendants and 8mm black rondelles to make five beaded pendant bails. For the necklace: Use a crimp bead (see page 5) to attach half the clasp to one end of a piece of beading wire, then string the beading pattern with evenly spaced pendants as shown. This design uses a mixture of black glass and stone rounds with large bicones and pendants, all interspersed with silver spacers.

(2) Beaded pendant bails make it easy to convert sliders into eye-catching pendants, like this red necklace: Cut a 6" length of 20-gauge fancy round antique brass wire and pass it through the upper loops (or holes) on the back of a slider. Pass through a gold spacer, 10mm red ceramic bead and gold spacer. Make a wrapped loop (see pages 10-11) to attach it to the center of a red suede cord necklace.

(3) You can also use beaded pendant bails to highlight ordinary round beads. For the turquoise ceramic earrings: Use 20-gauge gunmetal wire with 10mm rounds and antique gold spacers to make beaded pendant bails. Attach the bails to antique gold ear wires.

MAKING A BEADED PENDANT BAIL

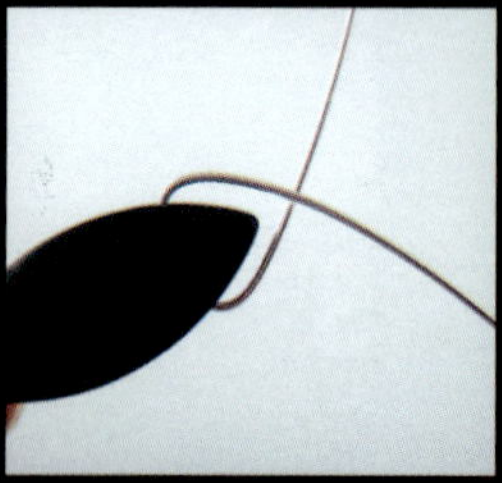

1 Cut a 6" length of wire and string a side-drilled bead onto the center.

2 Bend the ends in a right angle above the bead.

(4) Use beaded pendant bails to attach large stone chips and sticks. For each jasper earring, connect a beaded pendant bail with jasper stick and 3mm antique gold bead to each link on a 5-link piece of chain. Connect an eye pin to the top link, pass through an antique gold large-hole bead and 6mm garnet round. Make a basic loop (see pages 8-9) to attach it to an ear wire. Repeat for a matching earring.

(5) For the turquoise necklace, use 22-gauge gunmetal wire with 10mm rounds and 30mm stone pendants to make five beaded pendant bails. For the necklace: Hold two strands of gold beading wire together and use a crimp bead to attach half the clasp to one end. Then, pass both wires through a spacer. String a freshwater pearl onto each wire, then pass both through another spacer. Repeat this pattern for 2", then pass both wires together through alternating spacers and ceramic rounds. For the center section, pass each wire through a pearl, both through a pendant, each through a pearl, both through a spacer, each through a pearl. Repeat as shown, then complete the beading pattern so the necklace is symmetrical.

(6) The long, mixed metallic earrings use 22-gauge gunmetal wire to connect beaded pendant bails to wrapped loop links (see pages 10-11). The upper links use 3mm antique gold beads sandwiching 10mm faceted gray ovals. The middle links use copper bead caps sandwiching 10mm aqua ceramic rounds. The lower link uses 25mm stone pendants and 8mm gray rondelles.

Tip

You don't have to add the bead to a pendant bail. For a simpler wire hanger, wrap the extra wire from the upper loop downward over the top of the pendant.

Technique: MAKING A BEADED PENDANT BAIL

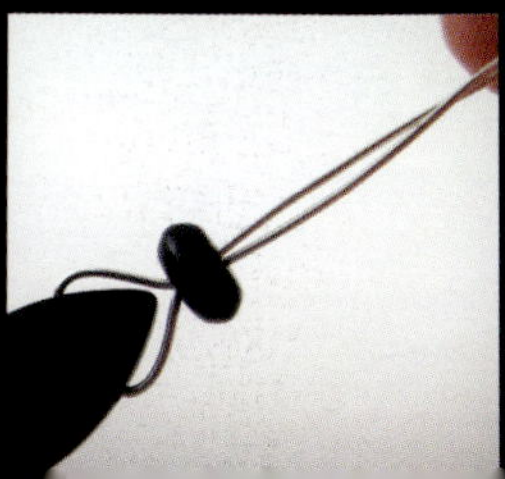

3 Hold the wires together and pass them through a bead (or beads).

4 Use one wire to make a wrapped loop, then trim off the other wire.

(1)
(2)
(3)

Circle PENDANTS

Beaded circles make attractive, eye-catching focal points for earrings and necklaces. Making your own pendant is a nice solution when you want to highlight special beads or when you want a pendant that echoes the look of your necklace. This is an especially great look for 8mm and larger beads.

(1) For the pink necklace: Make a circle pendant using 22-gauge wire, seven 12mm freshwater pearls and eight size 7 silver-lined clear seed beads. For the pendant hanger, attach an eye pin loop to the pendant loop. Pass the eye pin through: 6mm pink, spacer, pearl, spacer, 6mm pink and make a basic loop. For the sides of the necklace, use eye pins to link pink beads in various shapes and sizes together to the desired necklace length using basic loops (see pages 8-9). Attach a clasp to one end.

(2) The black/gray earrings show a more delicate variation of the circle pendant. Use 24-gauge hematite wire with 4mm crystal bicones and 3mm hematite rounds to make a circle pendant. At the top of the circle, pass through a black 7mm rondelle, hematite spacer, silver diamond-shaped bead and make a wrapped loop to attach it to an ear wire. Coil a leftover piece of wire around the ear wire to embellish it. Repeat for a matching earring.

(3) The multi-color earrings use faceted 8mm rondelles alternating with size 6 seed beads to make circle pendants from 20-gauge wire. At the top of each circle, pass the wire through a 6mm blue round. Make a wrapped loop (see pages 10-11) to attach it to an ear wire, then wrap the wire downward around the surface of the bead. Coil it around the base of the bead and over the coil at the top of the circle.

Tip

Use the thickest wire that will pass comfortably through the bead holes so the circle is strong and durable. For more delicate wire, make the circle smaller to reduce the possibility of bending it out of shape. In general, odd numbers of beads make for strong, balanced pendants.

1 **Cut a 10" length of wire, string alternating large and small beads onto a wire and cross the ends to form a circle shape.**

(4) For the green pendant: Use 22-gauge gunmetal wire with 10mm stone rounds and 4mm antique copper rounds. At the top of the pendant, pass the wire through a 5mm copper bead before making the wrapped loop. For the necklace: Use a crimp bead and bead tip to attach three 16" long copper beading wires to half of the clasp. Pass each wire through a stone chip, all through a copper spiral bead, each through a stone chip, all through a 5mm copper bead. Repeat the beading pattern until five copper spirals are strung, then string a chip on each wire and pass through the pendant. To complete the necklace, repeat the pattern in the reverse order so the necklace is symmetrical. Attach a clasp to one end of the necklace.

(5) Take a careful look at the purple necklace. The circle pendant is upside-down! The circle makes a pretty beaded hanger for the rectangle and tassel pendant. Use 13 stone 6mm rondelles with a 6" length of 22-gauge gunmetal wire to make a circle pendant. Slide a large-hole copper bead over the coil at the top of the pendant. Pass the wire through another rondelle, silver spacer, 22mm stone rectangle, copper spacer bead and make a wrapped loop. For the tassel, cut four 3" lengths of brown suede lacing and fold them in half. Hold the laces together and pass a 4" length of 24-gauge wire through the fold. Hold the wire ends together and pass them through: filigree bead cone, stone rondelle, silver spacer. Make a wrapped loop to attach it below the rectangle. To complete the necklace: Cut a piece of brown suede lacing to the desired necklace length, fold it in half, pass the fold through the circle pendant. Pass the lace ends through the fold and pull it taught to form a hanger. Knot the cord ends.

2 Bend the wires upward in a right angle. Coil one wire 3-4 times around the other, then cut off the extra wire.

3 Pass the wire through a bead and make a wrapped loop.

Technique:

MAKING A CIRCLE PENDANT

Layered PENDANTS

(1)

(2)

(3)

Buttons, filigree and other elements look so beautiful when stacked and layered! They have an artistic, vintage look that works well with chain, leather and beaded designs. A little bit of wire wrapping makes it easy to connect the components and use them in your jewelry creations.

(1) The gold/turquoise necklace uses a 22mm vintage, mother-of-pearl button for the base of the pendant. Layer a 6mm gold spacer and 15mm gold filigree over the button. Use 22-gauge gold wire with an 8mm turquoise glass bead, gold spacer and 4mm antique gold round to make a wire bail. Attach it to the center of a necklace chain.

(2) For the memory wire choker: Use a 3" piece of 20-gauge gunmetal wire to make a spiral (see page 14). Layer it over a 15mm gold filigree and 45mm antique copper flower. Use 22-gauge antique brass twisted wire with three copper spacers to make a wire bail. Attach it to the center of a gold memory wire choker. String a 3mm round bead onto each side of the pendant, then coil (see page 22) twisted wire around each side the pendant for 1". Use nylon jaw pliers to press the wire ends.

(3) The green necklace uses a 30mm olive green button as the base of the pendant. Layer an 8mm antique silver spacer over a 15mm gold filigree and 25mm antique silver filigree and place it over the button. Use 24-gauge twisted silver wire to make the wire bail, then pass the wire through a large-hole antique gold bead to cover the wrapping above the button. Pass through two stacked olive glass beads topped by a filigree bead cone. Use the doubled wire ends to make a wrapped loop. For the necklace: String the pendant onto the center of a 9" length of beading wire. String alternating glass and metal beads as shown. Crimp each wire end (see page 5) onto a length of chain to reach the desired necklace length. Attach a clasp to one end.

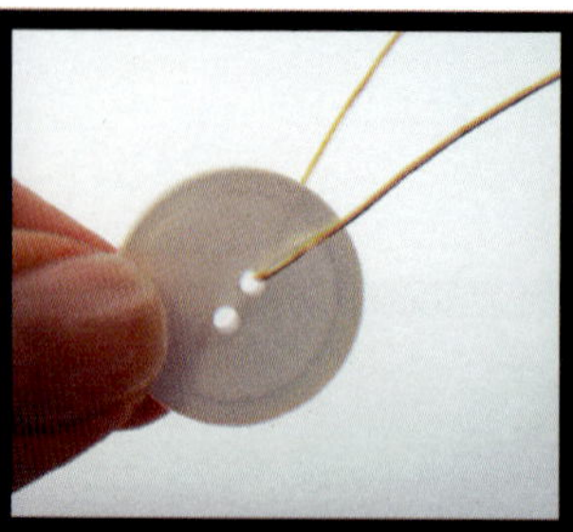

1 Cut a 6" length of wire and place it through a button or other component with about ⅓ extending from behind and ⅔ extending from the front.

(4) For the earrings: Layer a silver 8mm spacer over a white 16mm laser cut button and a 20mm antique silver square filigree. Use 22-gauge hematite wire with a 6mm crystal bicone and silver 5mm spacer to make the wire bail. Attach it to an ear wire. Repeat for a matching earring.

(5) The brown necklace shows how to put your own stamp on a large, eye-catching pendant. Layer a 5mm silver spacer over a 15mm antique silver filigree component. Use 20-gauge silver wire with a 6mm wooden round and 5mm silver spacer to make a wire bail by passing through a section of the pendant's cut-out design. Cut a 4" length of 20-gauge silver wire and make a wrapped loop on the pendant's original hanger hole, which is now positioned at the bottom. Pass the wire through a 6mm silver bead and make another wrapped loop to attach three 1½" chains. Attach the pendant to a brown suede lace necklace.

(6) For the silver/turquoise necklace: Layer a 5mm silver spacer over a 16mm turquoise disk and 40mm antique silver flower. Use 22-gauge twisted silver wire with a hematite spacer, 6mm turquoise round and silver spacer to make a wire bail. Make connected bead links (see pages 10-11) as shown for the focal section of the necklace, then add silver small cable chain to each end to reach your desired necklace length.

Tip

Like many wire projects, you can use any medium-large diameter of wire to create a wire bail for layered components. Choose the color and style that works best with the elements you want to layer.

2 Stack several elements, then bring the short wire forward and make a wrapped loop above the base component.

3 If desired, string beads onto the wire.

Technique: MAKING A WIRE BAIL FOR LAYERED COMPONENTS

Coils & CURVES

Coiling is one of the most basic wire techniques that you'll use again and again. Whether you coil wire around an ear wire to add a decorative element or you use coiling to attach beads to a bracelet, it's easy to make short coils by hand.

(1) For the turquoise necklace: Follow the steps below to coil 22-gauge wire around the edge of a 1½" solid ring for a half-inch. Pass the wire through a silver cube, two spacers, nugget, two spacers, cube and coil it around the other side extending toward the other end of the solid ring. Repeat for two more matching rings, adding spacers to fill the wire in the center of each ring if necessary. Make four 1" wire-wrapped rings without cubes and with slightly shorter coils. Use doubled 6mm jump rings to attach the alternating sizes of rings across the center of a necklace chain.

(2) The purple necklace features a large, 40mm stone oval bead with coils and wraps. To use the bead as a pendant: Cut a 12" length of 20-gauge wire and make a basic loop (see pages 8-9) on one end. Pass the wire through the bead, then make a wrapped loop and wrap the wire downward around the surface of the bead. Loop around the lower loop, then bring the wire upward across the front of the bead. Coil 22-gauge fancy round wire for ½" around the upper wire as shown, then secure it by coiling around the base of the upper loop. Mimic the look by coiling 22-gauge fancy round wire for ½" around a 1" solid ring as shown. Pass a head pin through an 8mm purple bead and make a wrapped loop (see pages 10-11) to attach the solid ring and dangle to the loop below the pendant. Use two jump rings to attach the pendant to purple suede lace of the desired length.

COILING WIRE AROUND A SURFACE

1 When coiling around a ring or other surface, leave a short tail so you have something to hold onto.

2 If your coil isn't as tight and consistent as you would like, use chain-nose pliers to carefully press the ends of the coil toward each other.

(3) The cuff bracelet combines the basic coiling/bead technique with some decorative wire wrapping over the surface of the beaded section. Cut a 12" length of 22-gauge hematite wire and coil it once around the bracelet to secure it. Pass back and forth across the bracelet, adding a bead and coiling on each pass. After you've added as many beads as will fit, pass back and forth in a diagonal pattern across the beaded section. Coil it to secure the end.

(4) You can also use coiling to add beads to the surface of an object. For the leather wrap bracelet: Cut a 12" length of 24-gauge antique brass wire and make a right angle bend ⅛" from the end. Hold the bent end against the inside of the bracelet, then coil over it three times to secure it. Pass through three 4mm mixed metallic rounds and coil three times over the surface of the bracelet. Repeat this pattern three times for each beaded section, spacing the sections about an inch apart across the bracelet.

(5) The red necklace uses coiling between beads on the pendant ring. Cut an 8" length of 22-gauge fancy round antique brass wire. Coil it two-three times around a 1" ring, pass through a red 4mm faceted stone bead and coil again to secure it. Repeat attaching seven beads evenly spaced on the ring. Use a 6" length of the same wire with a 20mm red lentil bead to make a decorative wrapped link (see pages 12-13). String a red 8mm carved stone bead and a 3mm antique gold bead onto a head pin and make a basic loop to attach the dangle and the wire-wrapped ring below the lentil bead. Use doubled 6mm jump rings to attach the pendant to a chain necklace.

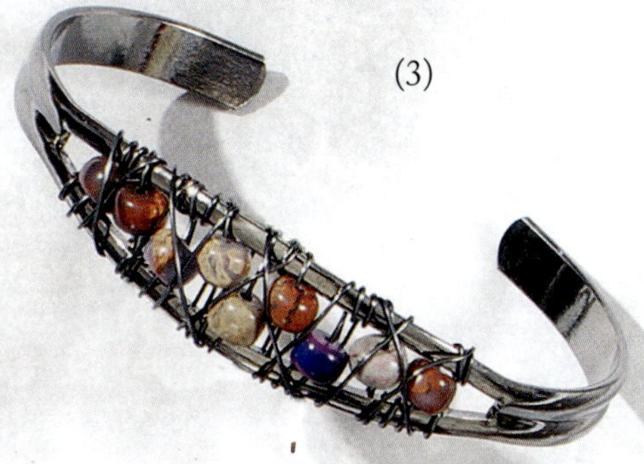

(3)

(4)

close-up of bracelet

(5)

Tip

It's easier to coil wire around a surface if you leave a tail at the beginning to hold onto as you wrap the wire. A half-inch length is usually sufficient. You can trim away the extra wire when you're finished.

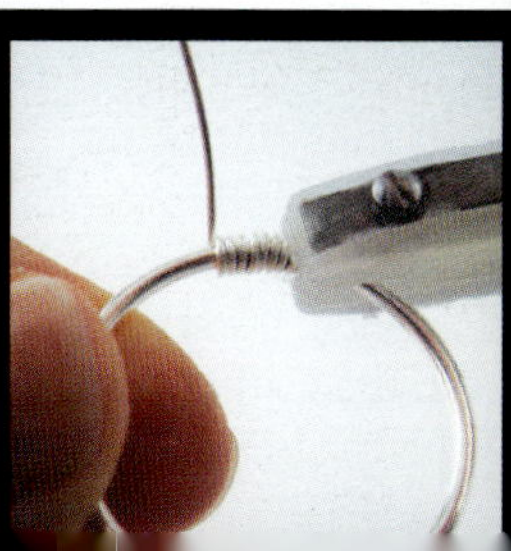

3 Use nylon-jaw pliers to press the cut wire end.

4 If you're adding a bead inside the frame, coil the wire end in the opposite direction to maintain balance on the frame

Technique:

COILING WIRE AROUND A SURFACE

MORE Coils & CURVES

(1)

2)

(3)

Long coils are simple to make when you use a coiling tool. I recommend making a lot of coils in a variety of sizes and colors. That way, you can pull from your stash when you're designing. It's a quick, convenient way to add a handmade look to many styles of jewelry, from bracelets to chokers, earrings and more.

(1) For the bangle bracelet: Use 22-gauge antique brass wire with a small mandrel to make a 4" coil. Cut it into ⅜" lengths. Cut two loops of bracelet memory that fit around the widest part of your fist. Make a basic loop on one end of each. Pass one memory wire through the upper loops on a slider and the other memory wire through the lower loops. Pass each wire through a 4mm antique gold round, coil, and three amber glass rondelles. Repeat the beading pattern four times as shown, then loop the memory wire ends to attach them to the corresponding beginning loops.

(2) Use hematite coils inside channel settings for a pair of mod-looking earrings. Use 24-gauge hematite wire with a small mandrel to make a little longer than 1" coil. Cut the coil in half. Pass an eye pin through one end of the channel, a long silver spacer bead (I wrapped these with wire for extra embellishment) and the coil. Pass outward through the upper hole and make a basic loop (see pages 8-9) to attach it to an ear wire. Pass a head pin through an 8mm stone bead, hematite spacer, silver spacer, a 4mm bead and make a wrapped loop to attach it below the rectangle. Repeat to make a matching earring.

(3) Who says a clasp has to hide in the back of a necklace? Make five connected wrapped loop links (see pages 10-11) using 20-gauge gunmetal wire with 14mm round beads that are sandwiched between silver bead caps. (Make the end loops slightly larger than the rest of the loops.) See the tip to make an "S" hook and connect it to one end of the links. Cut a piece of leather cord slightly longer than the desired necklace length. Fold it through the "S" hook and coil the leather cord together for half an inch. Use the same technique to attach the leather cord to the other end of the beaded links.

Tip

Make a loop at the end of a 2½" length of wire. Pass it through a 2" wire coil and make another basic loop. Use round nose pliers and your fingers to bend it into an "S" shape.

(4) Chandelier earrings feature delicate coils on each beaded drop. Use a small mandrel with 24-gauge copper wire to make a 1½" coil. Cut it into ¼" lengths. Pass a head pin through a 4mm bead and a coil, then make a basic loop to attach it to a loop on each chandelier finding. Repeat for each loop on the earrings.

(5) Short coils act as spacers in the magenta choker. Use a medium mandrel with 20-gauge wire to make a 4" coil. Cut it into ⅜" lengths. Make a basic loop (see pages 8-9) on one end of a 1½ loop memory wire choker. Pass the wire through: 6mm garnet round, spacer, 4mm hematite round, magenta nugget, 4mm hematite round, spacer, 6mm garnet, three spacers, 7mm magenta round, coil. Repeat the beading pattern in the reverse order. Continue this pattern to the end of the necklace, then make a basic loop.

(6) You can coil seed beads right onto the Coiling Gizmo, too. Thread green seed beads onto 24-gauge wire while it's still on the spool, then use a small mandrel to make a 3" coil. String it onto the center of a memory wire necklace. For the pendant: a. Connect a daisy charm to a 4mm jump ring. b. Pass a head pin through a 6mm crystal bicone and make a wrapped loop to attach it to the last link on a ¾" chain. c. Pass a head pin through a leaf bead, make a wrapped loop and attach it to an eye pin loop. d. Pass the eye pin through a 6mm bicone crystal and make a basic loop. Connect a 6mm jump ring to the top of each of these dangles. Cut 4" of 22-gauge wire and make a wrapped loop that connects the pendant and the 6mm jump ring. Pass it through a 10mm bead and make a large wrapped loop. Make a silver "S" hook (see the tip). String the pendant onto the lower loop of the "S" hook and use two 8mm jump rings to connect the upper loop to the center of the choker.

Technique: USING A COILING GIZMO

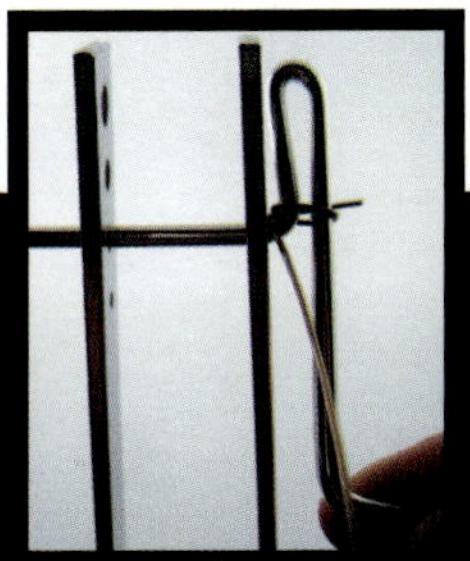

1 Leaving the wire connected to the spool, wrap the free end around the rod (or mandrel) to secure it while you coil.

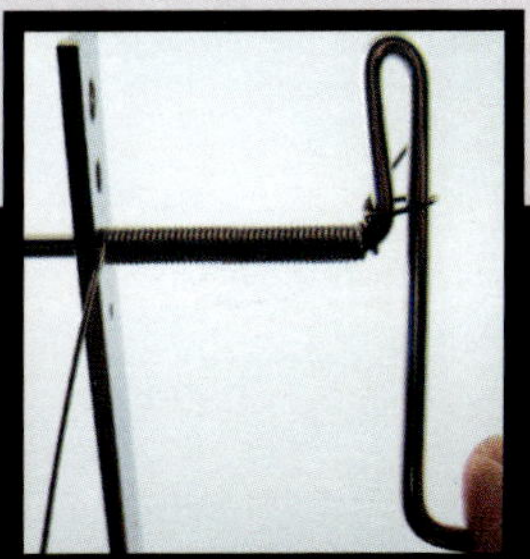

2 Hold the wire in your non-dominant hand to maintain slight tension while you use your dominant hand to turn the handle away from yourself to coil the wire on the rod.

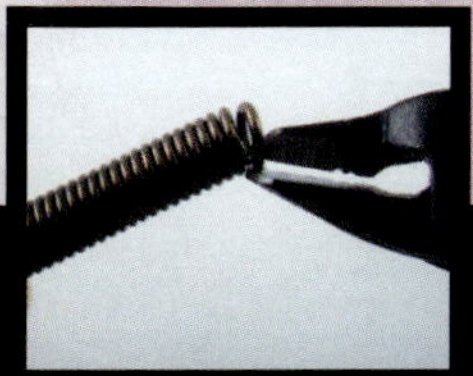

3 Cut the wire off the rod and trim off any sharp ends.

Bead & Wire FLOWERS

Three cheers for flower power! Bead and wire flowers make colorful, eye-catching focal points that can be layered together to create dramatic effects. Whether you make them in your favorite colors or use leftover beads from other projects, this technique makes it easy to create distinctive wire and bead flowers.

(1) Start out nice and simple with this basic black and purple flower pendant on a leather necklace. Follow the steps below to make a bead and wire flower using 22-gauge wire with five black 15mm flat teardrops and an 8mm purple lentil in the center. Spiral (see page 14) the ends on the back of the pendant. To hang the flower, pass the leather cord under a wire on the back of one of the petals.

(2) For the blue choker: Use five light blue 15mm flat nuggets and three dark blue 6mm faceted rounds to make a pendant with 22-gauge wire. String a beaded pattern in shades of blue onto a memory wire choker, then wrap the wire ends around the center of the necklace to connect it.

(3) The turquoise flower uses five 12mm flat ovals for petals with a 6mm freshwater pearl in the center. Use black, silver, white and turquoise beads with flexible beading to make a necklace, then attach a 4mm jump ring to the wire behind one of the flower petals. Connect it to another 4mm jump ring and position the top jump ring in the center of the necklace.

MAKING A BEAD & WIRE FLOWER

1 Cut a 12" length of wire and string a bead onto the center of the wire. Fold the wire so it meets at the base of the bead and twist the wires together

2 String a bead onto one of the wires, fold the wire and twist the wires together at the base of the bead

3 Continue making petals on each side of the first bead until there are five total petals. Twist the wires together

(4) You can layer three flowers of different sizes to create a dramatic impact. A 1½" ring provides the structure and gives you a surface where you can attach the flowers. For the black flower, use five 15mm flat nuggets with a 12mm white pearl coin. Coil the extra wire to opposite sides of the circle to attach the black flower centered in the circle. If you have enough extra wire, use one end to make a wrapped loop at 12:00. (If you don't have enough extra, simply add another piece.) For the clear flower, use five 12mm clear glass beads with an 8mm black glass coin and attach it at 4:00. For the white flower, use six 6mm freshwater pearls with a 6mm flower coin and attach at 7:00. Attach the pendant loop to the center of a chain necklace.

(5) For the pink earrings: Use 6x9mm crystal teardrops with a 6mm bicone and 24-gauge wire to make a bead and wire flower. Coil the wire ends around opposite sides of a 1" hammered ring with the flower positioned in the center. Attach a 3" piece of wire to the ring at 12:00, pass it through a 6mm rectangular bead and make a wrapped loop to attach it to an ear wire. Repeat for a matching earring.

(6) The purple and amber necklace has a free-spirited, casual look that I love. Use five 12mm amber glass beads with a purple 8mm lentil and 22-gauge hematite wire. Coil the wire ends at 10:00 on a 1½" solid ring. Cut a 15" length of wire and make a wrapped loop on one end. Coil the base of the loop around 12:00 on the circle and wrap the wire again around the base of the loop to secure it. Pass through a 6mm purple stone rondelle, wrap around the ring, and add another bead. Continue until you reach the bead and wire flower. Coil the wire around the ring behind the flower to secure it. String the pendant onto the center of a brown suede lace necklace.

Tip

When using teardrop and briolette style beads for the flower petals, make sure you twist the wire against itself. Don't twist against the pointed tip of the bead, which can break under pressure.

4 Bring one wire end to the front of the flower and add a bead (or a few beads) to the center. Wrap the wire to the back and twist the ends together again.

5 The way you finish the back of the flower will depend on how it's going to be used. I used a separate piece of wire to attach this one to a choker. If you're making a pendant and have a lot of extra wire on the back, form it into a flat spiral (see page 14) for a decorative touch.

Technique:
MAKING A BEAD & WIRE FLOWER

TASSELS are Tops

Tassels are simple to make and versatile enough to use in a variety of jewelry design styles. There are several ways to make chain tassels, but the basic principle is the same: Connect several chains to a wire loop and add a topper. Combine tassels with beads and other components to make stylish earrings and pendants.

(1) The mixture of metals on the flower necklace along with the vintage-inspired components gives the design a romantic feel. For the tassel: Cut a 6" length of 24-gauge antique brass wire and make a small wrapped loop to connect five 1½" chains. Pass the wire through the wide end of a bead cap, then through a 4mm antique gold bead. Make a wrapped loop to connect it to the flower pendant. For the pendant, see pages 20-21 for tips on layering components and making a hanger. Attach it to an antique gold chain necklace.

(2) For the pearl earrings: Connect five 1½" copper chains to an eye pin loop. Pass it through a large-hole hematite bead, 6mm pearl, copper spacer and 4mm hematite round. Make a wrapped loop to attach it to an ear wire. Repeat for a matching earring.

(3) The copper and purple earrings use a large-hole bead at the top of the tassel. Cut a 6" length of 20-gauge gold wire and make a basic loop (see pages 8-9) to connect three 1" copper chains. Pass through the gold large-hole bead, 8mm purple rondelle and 14mm copper coin. Make a wrapped loop to connect it to an ear wire. Use basic loops to attach two 4mm gold beaded head pins to each chain. Repeat for a matching earring.

Tip

To cut even lengths of chain without counting the links, place several chains on a head pin and let the ends dangle downward. Trim all of the ends evenly.

1 Gather several chains onto an eye pin or basic wire loop.

(4) The black/gray necklace uses Figaro style chain for an artistic, modern look. Use an eye pin to connect seven uneven lengths of chain. Pass it through a bead cone, spacer and 20mm black/white bead. Form a basic loop. Make two beaded eye pins and attach them to the pendant: 4mm hematite, bead cap, 6mm black, bead cap, 4mm hematite. Attach doubled chains to each side of the necklace for the desired length. Use a beaded eye pin to attach half of the clasp to each side of the necklace.

(5) The turquoise earrings use a larger chain to make a bigger statement. Connect three 1½" chains to an eye pin loop, then pass the pin through a 10mm bead cap, 14mm turquoise bead, 6mm spacer. Make a basic loop to connect it to an ear wire. Repeat for a matching earring.

(6) For the purple necklace: Connect 10 uneven lengths of small cable chain to an eye pin loop. Pass it through the wide end of a beading cone, then make a wrapped loop. Connect an eye pin loop to the wrapped loop. Pass it through: size 6 seed bead, spacer, 14mm ceramic round, spacer, seed bead. Make a basic loop. For the necklace: String the pendant onto the center of a beading wire that's the desired necklace length. String three alternating size 6 seeds and three silver rounds on each side of the pendant. String size 10 seeds onto the remainder of the necklace. Crimp to attach a clasp.

2 Close the loop to secure the chains.

3 Pass the eye pin (or wire) through the wide end of a beading cone.

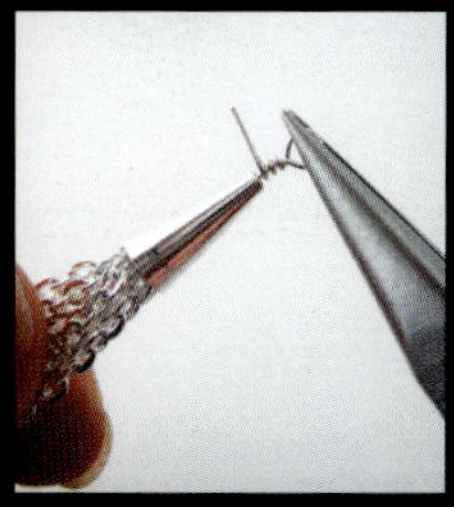

4 Make a wrapped loop outside the narrow end of the cone.

Technique:

MAKING A CHAIN TASSEL

Chic CHANDELIERS

Chandeliers never go out of style and it's easy to make your own for chic earrings and pendants. You can even turn them upside-down to make stylish statement necklaces. Check out the teal and red necklaces! The pendant hangers are chandeliers in disguise.

(1) Start out nice and simple with blue crystal chandelier earrings. To make the component, string four 4mm light blue bicones onto an eye pin. Bend the pin in a loop, then string four more beads and make a basic loop (see pages 8-9). Cut three chains to 1½", 1¾" and 2". Connect the ends to the lower loops on the chandelier component. String a 6mm dark blue crystal onto a head pin and make a wrapped loop (see pages 10-11). Use a 6mm jump ring to attach it to the top loop on the chandelier component. Attach the chandelier component to an ear wire. Repeat for a matching earring.

(2) Turn that chandelier component upside-down and use it for a pendant hanger! The heavy wire and tightly-spaced beads help the component keep its shape. For the teal component: Cut a 6" length of 18-gauge silver wire and make a wrapped loop on one end. Pass through eight teal/hematite 7mm beads and make a loop. Pass through eight more beads and make another wrapped loop. For the pendant: Pass an eye pin through a hematite spacer and 20mm hexagonal bead. Make a wrapped loop to attach it to the center loop on the component. Attach three 1" chains with beaded head pin dangles to the loop below the pendant. Attach medium curb chain to each side of the necklace to reach the desired necklace length. Add a beaded dangle to one end and a clasp to the other.

(3) For the red necklace, use the same technique as for the teal component, but cut a 12" wire length and use the extra wire in a decorative wrap (see pages 12-13) around the beads as shown. For the pendant, cut a 6" wire length and make a loose beaded spiral at the end (see page 14). Pass the wire through a 40mm stone teardrop, bead cap and 4mm crystal bicone. Make a wrapped loop to attach it to the center chandelier component loop. Attach Rolo chain to each side of the necklace to reach the desired necklace length. Use a beaded eye pin to attach each half of the clasp.

1 Fold the wire around round-nose pliers to make a loop in the center.

(4) For the stone earrings, follow the steps below to make each chandelier hanger using 22-gauge twisted antique brass wire with three 4mm rounds on each side. Attach one 1½" and one 2" length to the lower chandelier loops. Attach the upper loop to an ear wire. Repeat for a matching earring.

(5) The turquoise/gold earrings show you don't need to use a lot of beads to create a chandelier hanger. The wrapping technique is the same as shown below, but it uses 3mm antique gold rounds, bright gold spacer and ½" coil on each side of the component. Attach a 25mm beaded eye pin to the lower loops, along with three graduated strands of antique gold chain.

(6) You can also use a simple chandelier drop as a pendant, like this memory wire choker. It's the same basic technique as the blue earrings; using an eye pin with six 6mm stone rondelles to create the chandelier component. There are four lengths of chain for extra appeal. Connect an eye pin to the upper loop on the component, pass through a spacer, 8mm rondelle, bead cap and make a wrapped loop. String the pendant onto the center of a memory wire choker. Add a silver tube, seven stone rondelles, and two spacers to each side. Cover the remainder of the wire with seed beads and make a basic loop on each end.

Tip

For small components, you can use an eye pin. For longer components or for those made from special wire, you will need to make the component by hand (see the steps below).

2 Wrap one wire around the other to create a wrapped loop.

3 String beads onto the wire, then make a wrapped loop on the end.

4 Add beads and make a wrapped loop on the other end. Tip: If you don't add the chain before the loops are shut, you can open the end link of unsoldered chain and add it to the chandelier component.

Technique:

MAKING A CHANDELIER COMPONENT

Katiedids™ CREATIONS

Katiedids™ Creative Components make it simple to create your own wire-wrapped jewelry with a channel-set look. Mix different wire colors with silver components to make an artistic style statement with wire and 4mm beads.

(1) The aqua necklace features two round 5-hole Katiedids™ Creative Components that are linked together to make an eye-catching pendant. Cut 12" of 22-gauge silver wire. Make a wrapped loop (see pages 10-11) to attach it to a pendant bail. Pass inward through one set of holes on the channel component, wrap across surface, and add a 4mm stone bead. Continue wrapping and adding beads until you reach the lower holes. Cut another 12" wire, make another wrapped loop and repeat to cover the remainder with beads. Coil any extra wire around the base of the loop to secure them. Make another wire-wrapped component, attaching it below the first. At the bottom of the second component, pass through an 8mm rondelle and make a wrapped loop to connect seven 2" lengths of small cable chain. For the necklace: String the pendant onto the center of three silver beading wires that are 1" longer than the desired necklace length. Pass each wire through a 4mm stone bead, then pass all through a clear rondelle, repeating three times on each side of the necklace. Crimp the wires together, cover with a crimp cover, then braid to the ends. Crimp the braided ends together, attach a crimp cover and crimp to attach clasp.

(2) For the aqua earrings: Cut 16" of 22-gauge wire. Make a wrapped loop, pass inward through one end of a curved component and seven 4mm stone beads. Pass the wire outward through the other end. Make a wrapped loop. Wrap the extra wire in a criss-cross pattern across the curve. Attach ¾" chains to each side. Pass a head pin through: 4mm stone, spacer, 8mm clear rondelle, spacer, 4mm stone, and make a wrapped loop. Use a 4mm jump ring to attach the chains and beaded head pin to the ear wire. Add a crimp cover and coiled wire to the ear wire to embellish it. Repeat for a matching earring.

WIRE WRAPPING A KATIEDIDS™ CHANNEL FINDING

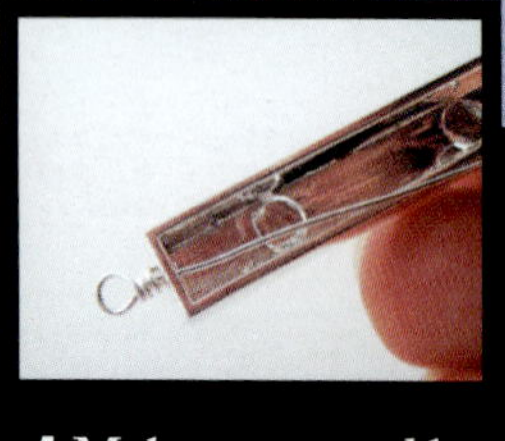

1 Make a wrapped loop on one end of the wire and pass it inward through the holes on the component.

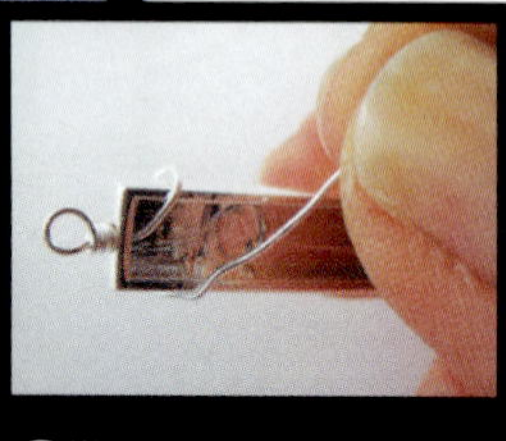

2 Wrap the wire around the back of the component and bring the wire end across the surface

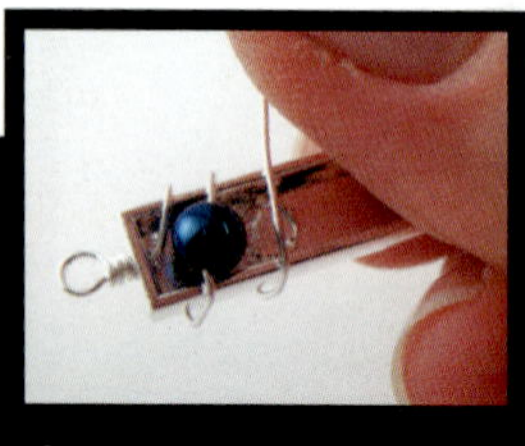

3 Pass the wire through a 4mm bead and wrap the wire around the component.

(3) For the pink earrings: Use 12" of 24-gauge twisted silver wire to make a wrapped loop. Pass the wire inward through the hole on one end of a curved channel, wrap it around to the front and add a 4mm crystal bicone. Wrap the wire around the component to secure it, repeat for eight beads. Make another wrapped loop. Attach a ¾" length chain to each loop. Pass a head pin through: 6mm bicone, spacer, 4mm bicone. Make a wrapped loop to attach it to a ¼" length of chain. Use a 4mm jump ring to connect chains to an ear wire. Repeat for a matching earring.

(4) The brown necklace mixes shapes and textures for a look that's right on-trend. Make two ⅜" coils (see page 25) from 20-gauge gunmetal wire. For the rectangle channels: Pass an eye pin through three 4mm ivory glass beads, coil, three ivory beads. Make a basic loop (see pages 8-9) . Cut 4" of 20-gauge gunmetal wire and wrap one end around the loop, coil the wire around the rectangle and secure it around the base of the opposite loop. Make four beaded eye pin links: ivory, 6mm spacer, 8mm bronzite, spacer, ivory. Make four eye pin links with three pyrite nuggets each. Connect two sets of links, then measure two sections of large link antique brass chain to reach the desired length. Connect the chains between the linked beads.

(5) For the blue earrings: Cut 12" of 24-gauge silver wire. Make a wrapped loop. Pass the wire inward through one end of the component and wire-wrap the component, adding seven 4mm rounds to the channel. Make a wrapped loop outside the opposite end. Pass a head pin through a 14mm teardrop bead topped with a bead cap then make a wrapped loop to attach it below the rectangle. Attach the upper loop to an ear wire. Repeat for a matching earring.

(6) For the agate earrings: Cut 16" of 24-gauge antique brass wire. Make a wrapped loop. Pass the wire inward through one set of holes on the channel component, wrap across the surface, and add a 4mm stone bead. Continue wrapping and adding beads until you reach the lower holes. Cut another 16" wire and make a wrapped loop at the end to connect three 1½" chains to the loop. Repeat to cover the remainder with beads. Coil any extra wire around the bases of the respective loops to secure them. Repeat for a matching earring.

Tip
Use beads in variegated colors to add natural visual texture to your channel set designs.

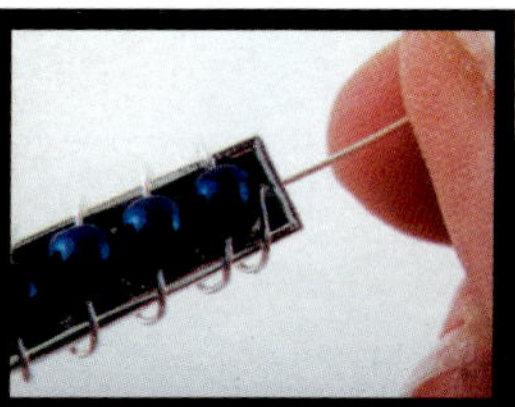

4 After you've covered the channel with beads, pass the wire outward through the end hole.

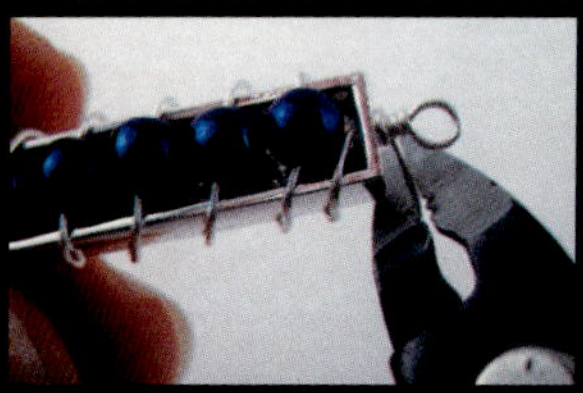

5 Make another wrapped loop, then cut off any extra wire.

Technique:
WIRE WRAPPING A KATIEDIDS™ CHANNEL FINDING

Tip

In addition to the necklace and earring ideas shown here, think about creating hair accessories, paper crafting embellishments and more with bead and wire branches.

This was one of the first decorative wire techniques I learned, and it's still one of my favorites. It has a delicate, intricate look that works beautifully with any bead style. This technique is especially popular for bridal jewelry – recreate any of these designs with pearls and crystals for someone's special day.

(1) For the green necklace: Cut 12" of 24-gauge wire. See the steps below to use these beads to create branches as shown: 25mm olive leaf, two 10mm olive rounds, two 8mm peridot rondelles (in the center), 8mm light green round, 12mm rectangle. Make a wrapped loop (see pages 10-11) to attach the beaded branches to a 1" hammered silver ring. Cut olive green suede lace to the desired necklace length, fold it in half and slip it through the ring. Place the cord ends through the fold and pull tight to fasten the knot. Attach eye crimps to the cord ends. Use jump rings to attach the clasp and extension chain.

(2) Although bead and wire branches make gorgeous linear pendants, you can wrap the branches onto any type of open ring, link or pendant. Use 12" sections of 24-gauge wire to attach red 4-10mm beads in various shapes to a 1½" silver ring. When one wire ends, coil the end around the ring and add another wire next to it. At the top of the circle, pass through: silver rondelle, 10mm ceramic round, silver rondelle, 4mm round. Make a wrapped loop to attach it to the center of a necklace chain.

(3) You can use this technique for earrings, too! Cut 12" of 24-gauge wire and use it with 16mm turquoise teardrops, four cloisonné rounds, and two 8mm rounds (in the center). Make a wrapped loop to attach it to an ear wire, then wrap the extra wire downward around the beads in a decorative wrap (see pages 12-13). Repeat for a matching earring.

MAKING WIRE BRANCHES

1 Center a length of wire through a bead and twist the wires together above the bead for ⅜".

2 String a bead onto one wire and fold it back by about ½". (You can vary this distance to create uneven branches.)

3 Twist the folded wires together.

Bead & Wire BRANCHES

(4) The bronze earrings have a cool, vintage style. Cut 10" of antique brass 24-gauge wire. Make three branches using 6mm brown faceted glass beads. Pass through: 10mm bronze faceted round, antique gold spacer, 6mm brown faceted. Make a wrapped loop to attach it to an ear wire, then wrap extra wire downward around the beads to make decorative links (see pages 12-13). Secure by coiling around the base of the lower loop. Repeat for a matching earring.

(5) For the gray necklace: Cut 8" of 20-gauge hematite wire. Make three branches using 8mm clear faceted rounds. Pass through a hematite spacer, 25mm gray oval, hematite spacer, silver size 6 seed bead. Make a wrapped loop. String the pendant onto the center of a memory wire choker. For the necklace: Pass through three 6mm faceted beads, 6mm hematite, hematite spacer, 8mm clear faceted, hematite spacer, 6mm hematite on each side. String 6mm faceted clear and size 6 seeds to cover remainder of wire on both sides of necklace.

(6) Black Artistic Wire® Mesh gives the crystal necklace a romantic, ruffled look. Cut 6" of 18-gauge wire and make a basic loop on each end. Bend it in a slight U-shape, then hammer so it will hold its shape. Cut 18" of 24-gauge silver wire and coil one end around the base of one loop. Twist wire and bead branches across the 18-gauge wire as shown. Coil the wire around the base of the opposite loop to secure it. Press the wire ends with nylon jaw pliers. For the necklace ends, use crimps to attach beading wire in the desired necklace length to each loop. Pass the beading wire through the wire mesh, then pull the sides of the mesh to ruffle it. Secure both ends with crimp covers. Crimp the ends and use jump rings to attach half of the clasp to each end.

4 String a different bead onto the other wire and create another branch.

5 If you want the center branch to look denser: Hold the wires together and pass them through another bead.

Technique: MAKING WIRE BRANCHES

Wirework SHAPES

A jig makes it easy to create your own wirework shapes to use as pendants, head pins, connectors and more. You can use a jig to make design motifs of all kinds. In general, you'll want to use thicker 18 or 20-gauge wire so your jigged components will hold their shapes.

(1) Jigs make it easy to make your own, decorative head pins. To set the jig for the blue earrings: Position two pegs with one hole between them on the center of the jig. On the next row down, position two jigs side-by-side. On the next row down, place one peg in the center. For the blue earrings: Cut 6" of 20-gauge wire and make a loop around the lowest peg on the jig. Make figure-eights back and forth across the remaining pegs, then make a right angle in the center. Pass through a 12mm blue bead, silver spacer, 4mm blue bicone. Make a wrapped loop (see pages 10-11) to attach it to an ear wire. Repeat for a matching earring.

(2) A clover-shaped link is an easy shape. Position the pegs in a square on the jig. Use 20-gauge hematite wire to loop around each peg, working your way around the square. Cut away any extra wire, then hammer the clover to harden it. Use a head pin with a basic loop (see pages 8-9) to attach a beaded dangle to the lower loop on the clover, then use a beaded eye pin with a basic loop to attach it to an ear wire. Repeat for a matching earring.

(3) For the purple necklace: Use 20-gauge gold wire to make two stacked figure-eights on the jig, then remove from the jig and form a loose spiral. Hammer the component, then pass the top wire through a gold spacer bead and make a basic loop. Stack the following beads on an eye pin: 6mm purple rondelle, gold spacer, 20mm purple rectangle, gold spacer, 6mm purple rondelle and make a basic loop. Attach the eye pin to the spiral component, then string the pendant onto the center of a memory wire choker. Add three size 6/0 seed beads to each side of the pendant and attach a crimp bead to hold the beads in place. Add a drop of jeweler's glue to each crimp to secure the beaded section.

(4) To make a simple charm holder, use the largest peg on the jig to make a circle with 18-gauge wire. Hammer the circle. Pass the wire ends through two stacked large-hole beads and make a wrapped loop to attach it to the desired length of wire mesh. Use wrapped loops to attach three beaded head pins to the circle.

Tip

If you're having trouble visualizing where to place your pegs on the jig, draw a pattern on a piece of graph paper and then position the pegs accordingly.

(5) For the gray figure 8 necklace: Position a medium peg above a large peg on the jig. Use 20-gauge wire to make a double figure 8 around the pegs. Turn one wire end in a basic loop at the intersection of the wires. Cut a 2" length of twisted silver wire and coil it around the other end at 3 o'clock on the lower loop of the figure 8 motif. Cut another 2" length of twisted silver wire and coil it around 9 o'clock on the upper loop of the figure 8. Use nylon jaw pliers to press the wire ends. Attach two beaded eye pin chain dangles to the lower loop and use beaded eye pins to connect the upper loop to a chain necklace as shown.

(6) Highlight a wirework clover inside a circle frame to create dramatic, tasseled earrings. Set up the pegs in a square pattern on the jig. Use 20-gauge silver wire to loop around each peg, working around the square. Cut away any extra wire, then hammer the clover to harden it. Connect an 8mm jump ring to each leaf on the clover and around the edge of a 1" hammered silver circle. Connect a beaded eye pin to the upper jump ring and attach it to an ear wire. Cut three 1¼" chain lengths and attach them to a 6mm jump ring. Connect the 6mm jump ring to the lower jump ring on the circle. Repeat for a matching earring.

(7) For the long silver pendant: Position a large peg in the center with a medium peg above and below. Use 10" of 18-gauge wire to coil around the pegs from one end to the other and around the center peg twice. Coil the lower wire around the top of the lower loop as shown and turn a basic loop to hang a beaded head pin dangle. Trim the other wire end at 10:00 on the middle circle. Cut 2" of hematite wire and coil it over the cut end of the wire at 10:00. Cut 6" of wire and make a wrapped loop on one end to attach it to the upper loop on the component. Pass through a 4mm silver round and a 25mm gray shell lentil, then make a wrapped loop and spiral the end in front of the bead (see page 14). Attach the pendant to the desired length of gray suede lace.

Technique: USING A JIG

1 Position pegs on the jig, then place the wire end into a hole on the jig and wrap the wire around the pegs.

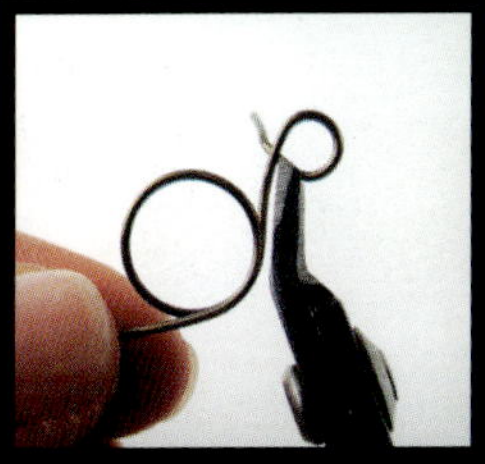

2 Remove the wire design from the jig and trim off any extra wire.

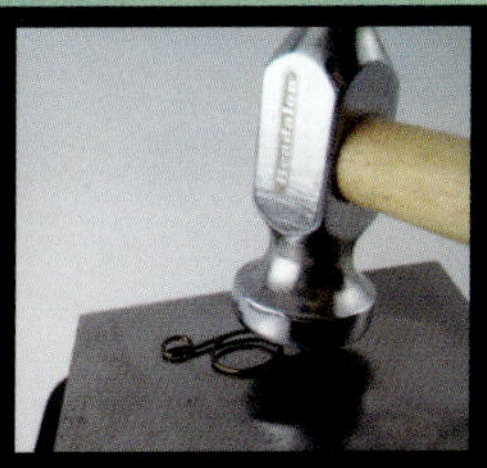

3 Place the wire design on a bench block (or anvil) and hammer it lightly to work harden the wire.

Caged PENDANTS

Caged pendants add a distinctive, handmade look to jewelry creations. Whether you make a large, eye-catching statement piece or small, decorative dangles, this technique is a great way to create your own pendants in any color scheme.

(1) The black and white pendant uses two colors of wire to mimic the bicolor look of the focal bead. Use 22-gauge hematite wire with a 20mm stone bead and 1½" circle to create the pendant (see steps below). Then, cut 12" of 22-gauge half-round silver wire and wrap it over the top of the hematite wire. For the necklace: Use 20-gauge silver wire to make two ½" coils (see page 25). Crimp (see page 2) to attach one end of a 16" beading wire to the clasp. Pass through 28 hematite 4mm rounds, 2 silver spacers, 6 black rondelles, 2 silver spacers, 6 black rondelles, 2 silver spacers, 6mm white round, ½" silver coil, 6mm white round, 2 silver spacers, 3 black rondelles. String the pendant, then complete the necklace in the reverse order so it's symmetrical.

(2) The earrings use teardrop beads in a whole new way! The caged pendants give them an edgy, artistic look. Use 24-gauge antique brass wire with 14mm beads and ⅞" silver rings to make two similar dangles. (Don't drive yourself crazy–they don't have to be identical.) Attach a 1" length of chain to the top of each pendant and connect it to an ear wire. Repeat for a matching earring.

(3) For the blue necklace: Frame an 18mm glass coin inside a 1" hammered circle. Use 20-gauge wire for a more intense wire look. (Because of the wire gauge and the tight fit, this one is a little harder to wrap. If you want a more delicate look, use a thinner wire gauge.) String the pendant onto the center of a beading wire that's the desired necklace length, then add blue and silver beads to each side. Crimp the beaded section in place and crimp to attach the clasp.

MAKING A CAGED PENDANT

1 Coil the wire end onto a frame and pass the wire through a bead.

2 Coil around the opposite side of the frame, then pass the wire across the surface of the bead to an opposite point

(4) Create a different look by using an assortment of smaller beads instead of a large, single bead. The brown earrings use 24-gauge antique brass wire with 4-8mm glass beads and a 1¼" antique brass ring for the caged pendant. Cut 6" of wire and use it with a 10mm faceted bead to make a decorative bead link (see pages 12-13) at the top of the earring. Attach it to an ear wire. Repeat for a matching earring.

(5) You can even create your own circles for framing large beads. Use 20-gauge hematite wire to make a 6" wire coil (see page 25). Cut a single loop of bracelet-size memory wire and string the wire coil onto it. Loosen a few rings at the end of each coil and press the ends together to interconnect them. Cut 20" of wire and use it to cage the 40mm purple bead inside the pendant. Make the pendant loop over the spot where the coil ends meet. Attach the pendant to a necklace chain.

(6) Just keep adding beads to create this icy, layered pendant! Use 22-gauge silver wire with a 1½" silver circle. Wire-wrap a mixture of 4-8mm clear/frosted beads. If you run out of wire and want to add more beads, just attach another piece and keep going. Instead of using the wire to make a loop at the top of the pendant, attach an eye pin. Pass it through a 10mm faceted bead and make a wrapped loop (see pages 10-11) to attach the pendant to the center of a long, linked wire/bead chain.

Tip

There are special findings that make caging easier–they have notches in the edges–but the pendants here use a variety of plain circle frames to show how you can turn any circle into a pendant.

3 Coil the wire again to secure it.

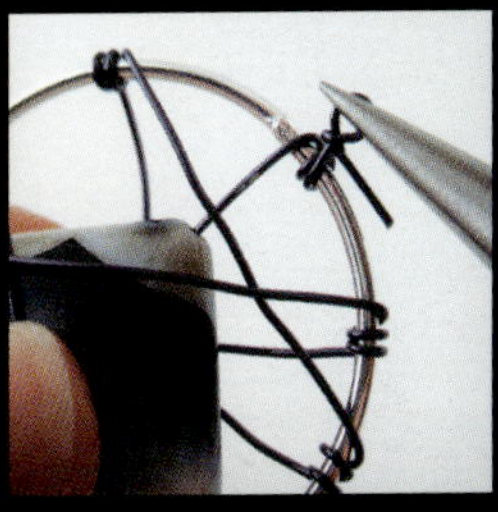

4 Pass back and forth across both sides of the bead, securing at various points on the frame. Make a wrapped loop at the top of the frame.

Technique: MAKING A CAGED PENDANT

(1)

(2)

(3)

Way Cool WIRE

Once you've tried your hand at wire wrapping jewelry, you'll start looking at all your craft projects in a new way! Here are a few ideas for adding wire embellishments to gifts, frames, ornaments and more.

(1) To decorate a pretty little package, cut a 12" length of 22-gauge gold wire and coil it loosely around a pencil. Slip it off and cut the coil in half. Make a basic loop (see pages 8-9) on one end of each wire to attach it to the back of a metal slider that coordinates with your wrapping. Tape the wire ends to the back of the package.

(2) For the picture ornament, mount a photo on paper or cardstock and center it behind a piece of thick, transparent plastic. (Sometimes you can find these with pre-made holes, if not, drill small holes in the upper corners and at the bottom center.) Cut 12" of 18-gauge wire and make a spiral on one end (see page 14). Pass it through the front of an upper hole, coil it loosely around a pencil except for the last inch. Pass the wire through the back of the other upper hole and spiral the end. Use a jump ring to attach a charm to the lower hole.

(3) I layered two painted and rubber-stamped pieces of wood together to create a little "dream" plaque. Cut 12" of wire and make a spiral on one end. Pass through a few beads, then coil it loosely around a pencil. Slip it off and continue adding a few more beads and coiling until you reach the other side. Pass it through the hole and spiral the end on the front of the plaque.

Tip

Create a loose, decorative wire coil by wrapping 20 or 22-gauge wire loosely around a pencil. For tight coils suitable for jewelry making, see page 25.